·COLLECTING·
The Passionate Pastime

·COLLECTING·
The Passionate Pastime

SUSANNA JOHNSTON & TIM BEDDOW

1817

HARPER & ROW, PUBLISHERS, New York
Cambridge, Philadelphia, San Francisco, Washington
London, Mexico City, São Paulo, Singapore, Sydney

1817

***HARPER & ROW, PUBLISHERS,** New York*
Cambridge, Philadelphia, San Francisco, Washington
London, Mexico City, São Paulo, Singapore, Sydney

COLLECTING: THE PASSIONATE PASTIME

FIRST U.S. EDITION

Printed in Great Britain

Library of Congress Cataloging-in-Publication Data

Johnston, Susanna.
  Collecting: the passionate pastime.

  1. Collectors and collecting – Great Britain.
I. Beddow, Tim.   II. Title.
AM343.J64   1987   069.4'0941   86-12050
          ISBN 0-06-015679-1

Frontispiece: An assortment of curios on James Reeve's desk.

*Title page: A selection of tea packets from the 1930s and 1940s
from Robert Opie's packaging collection.*

For Hugh Honour and John Fleming (SJ)
&
For my parents and Dominic (TB)

Above: A group of rare Territorial Infantry toy soldiers
from the collection of James Opie.

Contents

· CONTENTS ·

*Opposite: 'Seventh Heaven'. This part of the varied collection
at Snowshill Manor was perhaps Charles Paget Wade's favourite.
It contains many of the toys he had as a child before 1900.*

Foreword

—BAMBER GASCOIGNE—

Have you not often thought, after consuming the contents of some particularly bright or amusing packet, that if you kept such an object it would become valuable one day, one very distant day? There follows immediately a very clear impression of the resulting clutter, and after that brief chance of a reprieve the lovable carton passes on. How pleasant to discover in this fascinating book that someone (Robert Opie) has given house space, literally, to that familiar impulse and has accepted the domination of his life by rubbish. Once it has been collected, classified, catalogued and cherished by him, a transformation takes place. Those packages, refugees from a million dustbins, stand now revealed as an important slice of social history or of commercial art, depending on where your interests lie. The miracle has occurred. A great collection has been born.

There are two main categories of collector, the classifier and the hoarder. Mr Opie, in spite of the vast scope of his material, clearly ranks among the classifiers. Look at him on pages 92–3, among his serried ranks of biscuit tins. The slightest change of approach by Huntley and Palmer or McVitie and Price will be pounced upon with the excitement that a more traditional collector would reserve for an undescribed state of a Rembrandt etching.

By contrast the hoarder, jackdaw-like, will yearn for anything that may take his fancy. I first reacted strongly against hoarders when visiting a famous collection in Hyderabad, that of Sir Salar Jang, a potentate of the city in the late nineteenth century who could clearly resist nothing. I have little memory of his widely admired Aladdin's cave, extending to several buildings, except for a profusion of antlers, a huge glass case of briar pipes with the odd meerschaum, and an entire room in which pieces of china had been cemented to the walls. I was seized with claustrophobia and beat a hasty retreat, but I believe that somewhere in that vast Indian lumber room there must have been stuffed animals wearing clothes, for these have come to epitomize for me such mindless and airless accumulations. I am happy to assure you that there are no sartorial taxiderms in the pages of this book, though I would not give long odds against one or two of the assembled collectors falling for a winsome red squirrel in petticoats in later years.

The classifier has an eye and a soul that are the very opposite of the jackdaw's. As he progresses he will begin to perceive ever greater beauty in ever duller objects, which acquire an irresistible lustre precisely because they fill a gap – a gap predicted, very probably, by the process of classification, but even more exciting if unpredicted. Such a collection often becomes the basis for a book, and the test of collectorship will arrive when the book is complete. Does the interest survive publication, an event as final as the leaving of the last bus? If not, the collector stands revealed as a crypto-researcher, a character of less interest because the condition proves curable. I once thought I was a collector, of Richmond prints, but after writing about them I totally lost interest. A print that missed the book had missed the bus.

The luckiest collector-classifier is one whose quarry is newly collected (therefore cheap), is historically important and is intrinsically beautiful, and of this happy breed the best example in these pages is Sylvia Katz, whose book *Classic Plastics* was a glorious eye-opener when it came out in 1984. Since she pursues a material rather than a specific type of object, anything may become grist to her mill. Her book features calculating machines, furniture, jewellery, garments, crockery, clocks, games – you name it, they almost certainly made it. The research arising out of the collection is one of the great sources of pleasure to collectors, as these pages demonstrate again and again, and Sylvia Katz's researches take her into the history of technology, of design, of economics, of taste, and of much else besides. It was a blessed accident indeed that set her on her specialist path (an accidental beginning turns out to be another common theme), and it is a pleasure to read that in her case the event was a commission from a publisher. It is a creative profession after all.

Part of Christopher Petersen's collection of vintage cameras.

One of the subsidiary interests in meeting this endearing collection of collectors is to use them as a psychological litmus paper for oneself. Every reader will probably agree that the assembled addicts span the entire gamut from the admirable to the ridiculous, but there will be little agreement as to who is which. One can start, for example, by arranging them in sequence from the arch-classifier to the ultimate hoarder. At the former extreme must surely stand the collection with the least colour and the least variety, the milk bottles of Mike and Naomi Hull; at the other end of the scale is perhaps James Reeve with his 'curios'. Look at their respective pages (62 and 109). Which do you respond to? It will come as no surprise by now to learn that I get a positive charge of enthusiasm at the sight of all those rows of milk bottles (you can get the *idea* of the collection at a glance, but then the closer you look the more you become intrigued by the variations in detail), whereas a mere glimpse of the curios gives me more than a touch of the Salar Jangs. Others will have a precisely opposite reaction, and it is Reeve who stands in the older tradition of collecting. Early prints of collectors' dens commonly show a stuffed crocodile suspended from the ceiling or a rhinoceros horn propping open the door. As such a collection grows larger it becomes, like Alice, curiouser and curiouser. The other kind, that of the classifier, becomes clearer and clearer.

Let me leave you with the parable of the good and the bad hoarder, good and bad only in the sense of their merits as collectors. The bad hoarder was the neighbour of a friend of mine. He was a charming but somewhat dotty old man, so that when my friend was eventually asked inside his house he was prepared for it to be a little strange. Even so he did not expect to find one entire wall of the living room stacked high with empty cigarette packs, all identical, tied in bundles of ten. 'What', asked my friend, 'do you use those for?' 'To tell the truth,' replied the old man, with a look which in another context might have passed for cunning, 'I haven't actually found much use for them yet.'

That was a bad hoard in that it would never, even under the most favourable conditions, mutate into a collection. The good hoard was in its origin perhaps less endearing. It was compiled by a man who lived most of his life in the same house in Clapham. He was a loner, so much so that it was some weeks after his death before neighbours noticed a lifelessness about the house and called the police. They broke in to find the place stuffed from floor to ceiling with paper. For nearly half a century the man had subscribed to magazines and journals on a variety of subjects, throwing none of them away and so accidentally providing complete runs of by now very rare material. Most interesting of all were the glossy fashion magazines because from one of these each week he had ordered an expensive pair of high-heeled ladies' shoes, as advertised. The shoes had been taken out of their boxes, worn perhaps once or twice round the house, and then replaced in mint condition. Here was a hoard which was instantly transmogrified, by the mere light of day, into a costume collection of extreme importance. It has gone to a larger home where it is more widely appreciated – the Victoria and Albert Museum.

The moral? There is hope for us all. Clearly we should cherish any modest peculiarity we can lay claim to, and we may turn out to have been collectors after all.

Introduction

—SUSANNA JOHNSTON—

The word 'collector' may convey the image of some privileged fellow, a mainstay of auction houses throughout the world, who has been rich or shrewd enough to amass a large number of works of art.

Indeed such treasure stores exist, but the habit of collecting a miscellany of objects is most certainly a pastime within the reach not only of the wealthy and worldly, but of every human being. Collectors of pebbles, cigarette-cards, badges, buttons and pressed flowers illustrate this fact time and again. Even in the most modest of homes people collect – anything from sea-shells and crested china to pottery and brass. Even the archetypal stamp-collector can thrive on the swap system and a bit of luck.

The urge to acquire is a strong one and, in spite of Dr Johnson's example in his definition of the word, 'the idle acquire weight by lying down', most people who acquire do so with an energetic passion.

Collecting, as in the cases of Lady Diana Cooper and her unicorns, Lady Lambton and her butterflies and the owners of toast-racks, teapots and corkscrews by the thousand, can be a hobby. In other instances it can be an obsession and in some a downright mania.

It is not difficult to identify with the primitive urge to collect, whether from necessity (for example, the gathering of twigs to light a fire) or for pleasure since there must always be a thrill when the eye lights on an object that it seeks.

In Britain there is a true talent for the more developed stage of this primitive instinct and, when the cobwebs have been brushed away, dozens of unusual, bizarre and even eccentric collections can be found around the country.

The collecting urge is often triggered in the nursery by the arrival of an unexpected present or by a particular experience: the gift of a foreign doll, perhaps, or a visit to a museum. Children are often obsessive collectors, whether of conkers, lead soldiers, Dinky toys or coins. Some children have a desperate urge to rescue. One girl we met owns to having about five hundred teddy bears, many of them plucked from off the backs of dust carts. She just couldn't tolerate seeing them discarded or abused. Many of the collectors who appear in this book have said, when referring to a favourite treasure, that 'it was crying out to be saved'.

Sometimes this early excitement can develop into a lifelong interest, as it has done for Sir Patrick Wall and his model ships and aircraft, or for Mervyn Mitton and his police impedimenta. Sometimes it can come to dominate the entire life of the collector and become an academic absorption as it has done in the case of Robert Opie and his consumer goods, Charles Brooking and his architectural fragments or Gerald Wells and his vintage wireless sets.

Parents have been driven wild when, trailing children round some major European city in the hope of instilling a little culture into them, it has transpired that all they are interested in is collecting the various types of sugar packets from *pensione* dining-rooms.

In the world of adult collectors, there is, perhaps, a small reluctance to relinquish the toys of childhood and the fantasies that go with them. Part of the pleasure lies in the continuing to tend, polish and arrange without the danger of being considered, or of considering themselves to be quite cranky. A form of contentment can come from the privacy of being involved in an occupation that few others can understand.

An article that appeared anonymously in *The Times* on 12 August 1910 puts forward some interesting theories:

The collector's instinct seems to be a curious by-product of the human mind; and not only of the human mind, for monkeys, magpies and even dogs sometimes have it. When a dog makes a store of bones, old and entirely fleshless, he is like the collector who keeps things because they are obsolete. A used postage stamp is to a man what a bone without flesh is to a dog: but the collector of postage stamps goes further than the dog, in that he prefers an old postage stamp to a new one, while no dog, however ardent a collector of bones without flesh, would not rather have a bone with flesh on it. There is more method in the human

Some interesting truncheons from Mervyn Mitton's collection of British police equipment,
including a William IV Special Constable's truncheon from Cardiff.
The white helmet, dating from the 1930s, belonged to the City of London police.
The Wedgewood plate commemorates the 150th anniversary of the Metropolitan police.

collector, however, since he always has before him the ideal of a complete collection, whereas no dog, probably, ever dreamed of acquiring specimens of all the different kinds of bones that there are in the world. The ideal of the complete collection is the usual spur of the human collector; and often he will collect the most out-of-the-way things in the hope of attaining it. But there is also the spur of rivalry, and because of that there are not many collections of things that no one else collects.

It has also been suggested that the obsessive instinct to collect is peculiar to the Anglo-Saxon island race. Continentals, apparently, don't go in for match-box labels or beer mats to anything like the same extent. The largest collection of beer mats in the world, according to the *Guinness Book of Records*, is owned by a man in Glasgow and totalled 15,717 at the last count. The fact that we have been looting and conquering islanders may have some relevance: sea-captains and army officers have often returned to a safe and unconquered country with foreign trophies. We have always had somewhere secure to bring things back to, and this may help to explain the mysterious phenomenon.

In this book we have visited a number of collections and we have tried to make a varied selection. They are not necessarily all definitive in their areas. We have made our choice for many reasons: the validity of the objects, the effect they have had on the lives of their owners, and the approachability of the owners themselves to whom we owe much gratitude for allowing us to visit them and share their personal interests.

Often we have come up against the problem of owners who have concentrated much of their lives on assembling a sensational display only to wonder later, 'What will happen to these things when I have gone?' Few people could be expected to give house room, at short notice, to 35,000 toy soldiers, 8,000 models of ships or 5,000 truncheons. Not many museums have the space for the sudden challenge of a complete collection.

Whatever the underlying reasons for collecting, there is no doubt that those afflicted with the craze lead exciting lives. There is a great deal of enjoyment to be had in the pursuit of elusive bargains.

Charles Rowed, a passionate collector of antiques in the early part of this century, wrote:

I attempt no estimate of the miles I have travelled in pursuit of the game. I have motored as far north as Dunbar with success, made discoveries in Dover, found dishes in Devonshire, turned up treasures when touring the Lakes and been over to Ireland for pewter. Reflections on these journeys are constantly arising as my eye lights on one or another of the numerous specimens which adorn my home and I am truly thankful that I have turned to the collecting of antiques in the way I have done, thereby providing myself with a pastime which has been beneficial to the body and mind of a busy man.

Experts are baffled by a mania that can take hold of common-sense – by the mental foundations on which the craving to collect is based. How, in later life, do earlier associations influence these particular fancies? Is the craving inherent, or do circumstances and environment create it? One doctor friend diagnoses collecting as a disease on which he considers himself to be an authority, if not a specialist, since his knowledge has been acquired by constant practice. His faculties are so acute that on one occasion, while feeling the pulse of a patient, he lost count of the beats through catching sight of a Bartolozzi print hanging near the bed. He is pleased to say that the patient recovered and that he himself obtained the print. And some psychiatrists propound that collecting is connected with constipation – that it all goes back to potty training. Sigmund Freud, for example, held that where a child had obtained gratification by refusing to cooperate with its mother in the matter of toileting, this would be translated in adulthood into a tendency to hoard, withhold and (by implication) to collect. There are others who would recommend taking this theory with a dose of salts.

Antique Woodworking Tools

—TONY BARWICK—

Tony Barwick has a unique approach to collecting antique woodworking tools – he prefers to build small specialist collections rather than one large one. He owns a woodworking tool shop in Upper Street, Islington, where the constant turnover of stock gives him an ideal opportunity to handle tools that date, in some cases, from Roman times, though others are more modern.

He has a truly commercial attitude to collecting and does not find it difficult to dispose of his collections. 'I prefer to put together a collection, say, of eighteenth-century English moulding planes, learn as much as I can from it and then pass it on to another collector, just retaining a few items for future reference. This gives me the funds to look at another area of the field – at the moment it is hammers ranging from Roman to eighteenth-century.'

An upstairs room above the crowded shop contains Tony Barwick's personal treasure trove. 'Most people don't know about it. It's by invitation only that this room is opened up.' Here are planes from the South Seas, decorated Dutch planes of the eighteenth century, carved and decorated eighteenth-century musical instrument makers' planes, early saws, chisels, compasses and callipers. He applauds the fact that the decoration on these tools was unnecessary: 'It was done for the sheer joy of the craft, and each item, apart from being a functional tool, shows the craftsman's skill in what he uses to produce fine work. Look, on that plane there is carved a mythical creature that chews timber – highly appropriate. Most of these tools were made by craftsmen themselves. You're looking at a distinctive style as well as understanding the skill of the man who made it.'

Behind Mr Barwick, in his shop, are rows of moulding planes. Vices, saws, drills and other tools fill up every inch of available space.

assumed that only collectors would be interested. Over the years he has discovered that about 80 per cent of his clients buy his wares for practical purposes, often finding them cheaper, more comprehensive in range and better made than the average tool of today.

Individuals and museums collect anything from early planes (some in exotic woods) to compasses, saws, chisels and spanners. Tony Barwick goes to an enormous number of specialist auctions. At one he bought two-thirds of the items for sale. 'It really was the perfect type of sale for me – containing tools covering the entire range that I'm looking for, both for craftsmen and for collectors. But every time I scoop up a large batch, I almost have to redesign the shop around it. I'm still busy sorting out the residue of four auctions. Space is a terrible problem.'

Barwick regards himself as a collector in his own right – but the collection is only as an extension of his business. 'I'm not the sort of person to surround myself with an ever-growing pile of artifacts – I like to handle new things as often as possible. Buying and selling gives you this chance.'

'There is always the danger that tools will become fashionable and subject to the usual hype. And it is pretty understandable, as many are highly attractive, interesting artifacts. But the majority go out for use. There is a big and quite successful return to the crafts. Small businesses making good furniture and musical instruments, wood and stone carvers and shipbuilders are sprouting up all over the country.

'We have a new generation of good craftsmen with plenty going for them. There is a definite revulsion against utility goods, and more and more people appear to appreciate properly made and personally designed furniture.'

Barwick hires out tools for films, theatre, television and exhibitions. He is an expert and abhors seeing tools wrongly used on stage or screen. Coffin-makers in the television version of *Oliver Twist*, for instance, went in for some pretty serious wood-working solecisms.

Tony Barwick has been deeply involved in woodworking tools for fourteen years or more, and, in spite of the tremendously long hours and the sheer physical work involved in handling and selling the stuff, he loves it. Every day there is the chance that someone may walk into the shop with an exciting

Behind the old lathe are chisels and metal planes; adzes lean against the wall.

Tony Barwick is conscious of the aesthetic appeal of these craftsmen's tools, but it is the practical aspects of them that interest him most. When he looks at a nice piece of Chippendale, for instance, he likes to know what it was made with – what tools were used – and how certain problems were solved, and he links this information with the development of tools. He has always been interested in the functions of tools and owns a set of early planes used to make violins, maintaining that he is far more interested by them than he would be by a Stradivarius. 'There are more Stradivarius violins around today than there are the tools that went to make them.'

Tony Barwick was not at first aware that there would be a strong users' market for his tools. He had

A group of nineteenth-century metal planes

object, and every auction is still fun – 'Although', he admits, 'I don't like the paperwork, VAT and all the rest. I can't see the point of doing anything that you don't enjoy.'

Besides selling and collecting tools, Barwick also deals in books on a grand scale – 'Books on all the trades – from coalmining to, well, absolutely anything.'

Contentedly surrounded by exquisitely engraved seventeenth-century shipwright's callipers, by a particularly fine 1850 gentleman's tool-kit and by intricate tools for working ivory and hardwoods, he pauses to sell a strong chisel from the nineteenth century and an eighteenth-century ogee moulding plane. 'How about that? One a hundred years old

and the other two hundred years old, and still going off to do work!'

In the United States of America tool collecting is a big business. There are tool clubs with anything up to a thousand members, and the Tool and Trades History Society, formed a couple of years ago in Britain, has a large and growing home and international membership.

Tony Barwick accepts that 'there is something odd about collecting something very, very strange. I think the need to accumulate objects varies from person to person. Perhaps the word should be accumulating, rather than collecting. I think that you could, justifiably, read almost anything into the psychological motivation.'

Sewing Machines

—RAY BATCHELOR & JEFF GRACE—

Ray Batchelor and Jeff Grace live in West London with their red setter, Otto, and with about two hundred sewing machines. The passion for these machines was formed by Ray Batchelor in his youth, but now the concern is very much a joint one.

When Batchelor was eight he longed for a toy sewing machine. He asked his mother if he could have one for Christmas, and she agreed. The family used to celebrate the feast with young Ray's grandmother who, when she saw what was inside her grandson's parcel, looked at the boy's mother and said, 'What did you want to go and buy him a thing like that for?' She considered it 'sissy'. Ray's mother, in all honesty and with great confidence, replied, 'Well, it's what he asked for.'

Ray Batchelor played with the toy for a year or so, put it aside and went on to other things. Although this first toy gave birth to the interest, it lay dormant for ten years.

When he was eighteen and moved to his present flat with Jeff Grace, they looked about for bits and pieces of furniture and kept seeing (to their eyes, at any rate) 'beautiful sewing machines for around 50p apiece. They were considered to be junk.' The pair felt sorry for the old machines and began to buy. A friend had a machine that wouldn't work, so she asked Batchelor to look at it for her. At that stage he was not an authority on the subject, but he fiddled with it for three days and eventually got it going. Gradually, his childhood interest was reawakened.

Ray Batchelor started out in adult life as an actor, but, 'after "x" months of not doing much and of nobody doing much about my acting career', he thought that maybe he could make some money out of sewing machines.

'They were coming in thick and fast. We just couldn't resist them.' He opened up a small stand in the Portobello Road market. Not having done that

Opposite: Ray Batchelor and Jeff Grace in the room where their sewing machines are stored.
In the foreground is a 'Nelson's 70' – a lavishly decorated hand machine made by Jones for Nelson in the 1920s.

Above: A Jones hand machine made at Guide Bridge near Manchester in about 1895.
Many other companies already made machines of a similar design when Jones introduced this version in 1879.

sort of thing before, he didn't know the ropes. 'I was uncertain about how to begin. I couldn't very well call out "Fresh sewing machines". People came, but they looked a bit bemused. Then a dealer came along and bought the whole lot. He took them away in a taxi. I thought, "Great. This is my future life." But after that I never sold another one there and ended up with a stall in Shepherd's Bush Market which was only moderately successful.'

Batchelor confesses to not being much of a business-man. He could never bring himself to sell the nice machines and they began to accumulate. 'Initially we were very excited by quite ordinary ones. We still think they're wonderful.'

As their academic interest in the subject gathered momentum they started looking things up but found themselves confronted with a lot of false information. They could get so far and no further. Batchelor, who worked at the Science Museum, has been preparing a book on the subject for eight years. One reason for this is to spread knowledge of the sewing machine as widely as possible: 'Sewing machines in their own way are very important in the development of machine-tool technology. Guns, sewing machines and bicycles are generally lumped together. Nobody bothers to trace the links between them.'

By and large they have settled for domestic machines and, whenever possible, those in their original box containers and with their handbooks. A small back room is piled high with these wooden cases, each with a machine inside. Visitors often compare it to a morgue for animals – dozens of little cat-coffins!

In the sitting-room, several of the owners' favourite machines are on display. Beside the fireplace and supported by brackets is one they 'absolutely ached for'. It's called a Grover and Baker, and sews with two threads directly from cotton reels so that it produces a sort of knitted seam. It was a domestic machine of its day and its date (1868) can be traced from the serial number. The proud owners had despaired of ever finding one. One day, at a time when Batchelor was running his business in a shop ('a complete fiasco'), a man came in and said, 'I've got this old embroidery machine. I was going to throw it out.' Batchelor bought it on the spot, and ran, carrying it in his arms, to the place where Grace was working at the time. Grace looked at it and said, 'Whee-e-e-e!' They waltzed round a room full of people with the machine between them. Grace's workmates thought they were crazed, 'and we probably were, but a Grover and Baker is something special; the machine that you have to have in order to prove that you're a respectable sewing machine collector'. Batchelor emphasizes that 'sewing machines come in a far wider variety than most people think. Wonderful things.'

In his book, Ray Batchelor aims to persuade the public that sewing machines are varied and interesting. He resents the fact that the name Singer alone leaps to the mind of ignorant people and has eclipsed and overshadowed other makers and inventors in sewing machine history. He recommends a book by Ruth Brandon on Singer, the man. Singer was a maverick; he had four or five wives in different parts of New York, ran them all concurrently, and swindled his business partner. He was a showman, a failed actor and, although he sang 'The Song of the Shirt' to music while promoting his invention, he despised the sewing machine.

Batchelor and Grace are often asked if they ever put their machines to any practical use. The answer is that, apart from making sure that they work, they don't use them much. Batchelor did once get out his Wheeler and Wilson (which sews from left to right) and made some shirts on it, but found it rather too time-consuming.

Churchilliana and Other Commemorabilia

—THE MARQUESS OF BATH—

On the top floor of Longleat House, perhaps the most perfect example of high Elizabethan architecture still standing, is a road sign, at right angles to the wall, that reads: 'Churchill 1½ miles'. The sixth Marquess of Bath draws attention to it. 'That, I'm sorry to say, I stole. Stole it with a friend somewhere off the Axminster Road. We were both drunk at the time. Ten years ago at least. I don't think they'll get us now.'

The stolen sign leads visitors to the Bishop Ken Library, a room that twists and spreads over the top floor of one side of the house. In 1688 Thomas Ken, Bishop of Bath and Wells, was imprisoned in the Tower of London with other bishops for forbidding James II's Declaration of Indulgence to be read from his diocesan pulpit. Three years later he was deprived of his see for refusing to take the oath of allegiance to William and Mary. The first Viscount Weymouth, a friend of Ken's since his Oxford days, took pity on him and prepared these rooms for him at Longleat. Ken lived there for twenty years, and it was in this library, where the present Marquess

Above: Lord Bath on a velvet-covered sofa next to a Marno Hornak effigy of Winston Churchill.

Lord Bath's collection of Churchill stamps – considered to be the finest in the world.

Another effigy of Winston Churchill, seen here with his painting equipment, especially designed for the room by artist, Marno Hornak.

houses his incomparable collections, that he wrote the time-honoured hymn, 'Awake my soul and with the sun'. These apartments are not normally open to the public but can be viewed by appointment.

Lord Bath, as well as preserving his inheritance, has greatly embellished it. His son, Lord Christopher Thynne, describes his father as 'an ardent collector. With so much behind him – books, pictures and so on – I think he felt obliged to add something during his lifetime.'

The first among Lord Bath's private collections was late-nineteenth-century children's books. There are rows upon rows of first editions (Kate Greenaway, Beatrix Potter, Lewis Carroll, Walter Crane, Conan Doyle, Mrs Molesworth), many with their dust-covers still intact.

From these shelves you turn to the east end of the library which looks out across Capability Brown landscaped lakes to wooded parkland and up to 'Heaven's Gate', the celebrated beauty-spot.

In the foreground, on a velvet-covered sofa, sits a larger than life-size, cigar-smoking effigy of Winston Churchill, dressed in a red siren-suit. Not far from this, also seated and equally lifelike, is a similar figure wearing a blue denim siren-suit. The blue-clad fellow is hard at work with his paintbrush, adding a finishing stroke to a portrait of Doris Castlerosse. Both the painting and the frame are original. So are the siren-suits. The two figures were specially made for the room by artist Marno Hornak.

Lord Bath explains: 'When Churchill died, his secretary wanted to throw these clothes out. She came down the back stairs with three of these suits. When she saw the under-gardener she said, "You might like to cut these up for your children." He didn't cut 'em all up but unfortunately he did cut up the purple one. I got the other two. Also his spectacles. She was going to throw those away. I don't understand that.' The spectacles nestle in their original case beside a letter from the under-gardener vouching for their authenticity, and for that of the siren-suits.

Lining the walls at this end of the room are Churchill's books ('pretty well all signed'), Eddie Marsh's

letters from and to Churchill, framed maps, stamps and charters. Below these, in glass cases, are stored innumerable treasures with a Churchill connection: toby-jugs, arm-bands worn by ushers at his funeral, Churchill's birthday book, even his luggage labels, and, according to Lord Bath, 'they keep coming in'. There is a lap-rug belonging to the great man, and his passport – 'A very important piece. I can't remember how I came by it. Such a long time ago.'

Among busts and photographs, one of Churchill's cigars, half smoked, lies in state. 'My cousin got that for me. She was playing a game of bezique with him and he had to go to the lavatory. She stubbed it out and put it in her pocket. It's all down there on paper to prove it. No point if there isn't proof.'

Lord Bath's collection of Churchill stamps is the finest in the world. Every inch of wall space is covered with them. Beneath them in further showcases are bits and pieces of 'rubbish', as Lord Bath calls them: Churchill biscuit tins and tea-caddies; and (very definitely non-rubbish) hundreds of Churchill medals of bronze, copper and gold. 'I had a hell of a job getting that Cuba one,' the owner remembers. 'Another medal I couldn't get was the Senior Service one of America. They don't sell their medals there.'

After the Churchilliana comes the Hitler collection. At the back of this small room stands the black-clad figure of Adolf Hitler, also made for Lord Bath, with blood-curdling skill, by Marno Hornak. Behind him hangs a mock-up painting by Dame Laura Knight of the Nuremberg Trials, and alongside it paintings by the Führer; not in themselves particularly distinguished, 'but,' says Lord Bath, 'it's unexpected that a man who did what he did should have had a paintbrush at all.' The room is full of 'Nazi stuff' – an SS chair, swastikas, coins, arm-bands and ornamental flags embossed in gold and silver. 'Extraordinary, really, that a country like that, a derelict country in 1935 with no money, should have produced all this.'

Lord Christopher fiercely defends his father against charges of mawkishness, maintaining that 'the Hitler collection is simply an offshoot of the Churchill one. My father was a great fan of Churchill. He began to collect the Hitler stuff because so much

Opposite: In the small chamber devoted to Hitleriana – a life-size figure of the Führer,
also made for the collection by Marno Hornak.

of it tied in with Churchill. Most of the Hitler "objects" have been given to him. People don't know what to do with some of the horrible things – master keys of Belsen and a rubber truncheon, for example. They think, rightly, that they represent history and shouldn't be thrown away, but don't want them in their houses either. "Longleat can have them," they say. Things that are black or creepy tend to be sent along to our suitable repository.'

A wine bottle stands on the table. 'Yes,' says Lord Bath, 'my wine merchant said that he'd got a bottle of wine of the Hitler period, 1933; swastikas and everything. He said that I could have it but he sent it along empty. That annoyed me. He should have sent it with the wine in it.

'Now. That match-box. That's terribly valuable. Americans want it galore. It was made in the village where the whole movement started. Junk becomes very valuable just *because* people throw so much of it away.'

As a backcloth to these creepy relics hang Belsen posters showing victims by the thousand dying of starvation, 'just to remind people that Hitler is not to be glorified'.

Edward VIII has also been allocated his own small room which is a-glitter with souvenirs commemorating the uncrowned king. In one corner stands a letter-box carrying the royal coat-of-arms. 'They had all been put out in the streets. They had to take 'em down again.'

Cupboards bulge with Edward VIII shoe-trees, bread-knives, plumes and feathers. On the window-sill stands one tall shiny boot. Lord Bath recalls going off 'to buy a pair of shoes, you see. I got talking to Mr Maxwell, Dover Street I think it was – or Albemarle – I can't remember which. He didn't know who I was. It suddenly came to me to ask him, "Have you anything of the Prince of Wales', sir?" He said, "Yes. I've got a pair of hunting boots." I asked if he'd sell 'em to me. He answered, "No. I can't sell them to you because they're of great interest to Americans." I said, "But you haven't got a label or anything on

'em." But he replied that he liked to point 'em out – so I asked if he'd sell me one. He said, "All right. I might do that. It won't fit anybody else." He asked me for ten shillings. I gave him a quid. I ought to have given him a fiver, I suppose. The Prince of Wales never wore 'em. He declined to accept delivery of the boots because the feet weren't long enough to emphasize the slenderness of his legs. Henry Maxwell and Sons. That's what they were called. They've gone now. I would have bought the other one if I'd known.'

Even at Longleat there are problems of space. Edward VIII tea-strainers and babies' rattles are squeezed in beside Royal Doulton busts and made-up jig-saw puzzles – one of the Prince in military uniform, another in a Fair Isle jumper carrying a little Scottie dog. There is a splendid model of him in coronation robes which, of course, he never wore. 'My son Christopher gave me that as an eightieth birthday present. Marvellous.'

Lord Bath is very fond of his Windsor collection, 'although the Duke did give me the sack. I was meant to be involved with the running of the Duchy of Cornwall. I never opened my mouth. I was terrified of royalty. None of us ever went down to look at the Duchy in those days and it was quite difficult to say what should be done and what shouldn't. So I'm afraid he said I must go. It was a nasty feeling. I'd never been sacked before. Horrible – even though I deserved it.'

In another part of the great library there is a nook dedicated to Mrs Thatcher. 'I'm a Tory,' Lord Bath insists. 'I'm a supporter, but that's not why I collect her. I collect her because she's the first woman to be Prime Minister of England and she's bound to be famous. She's famous already, of course. Some of these are not very pretty, I'm afraid.' He points at a pair of rubbery masks, which are unfair but unmistakable, and adds, 'It'll all get broken one day, I expect, on this table. No more cupboards or shelves. I did think of collecting the present Prince and Princess of Wales, but it would be too big a job. It would kill me, I think.'

Opposite: Commemorabilia relating to Edward VIII

Steam Locomotives and Rolling Stock

—THE REVEREND E. R. BOSTON—

The Reverend 'Teddy' Boston runs his own personal steam museum in the Rectory garden at Cadeby in Leicestershire. He opens it to the public 'whenever they want to see it', and organizes a regular service for passengers on the second Sunday of each month (an announcement that has a suitably ecclesiastical ring).

The Rectory garden is completely occupied by rolling-stock and locomotives, wagons and open trucks, giving the impression of a gypsy fairground. Visitors can shunt round the garden, the Rector at the throttle, through dense and prickly holly trees, past a sharp bend and on towards the nearby graveyard. Railway signals wink out from among the trees, and signs warning that 'Passengers must not cross the line', as well as lanterns and lamp-posts, are propped up along the route. Steam and whistles are familiar to the inhabitants of the small village of Cadeby, and no parishioner shows surprise at the sight of the vicar cleaning out 'Pixie', his first and favourite engine, within feet of the churchyard. Mr Boston visited the local quarry office in 1961, caught a glimpse of Pixie, a two-foot-gauge Bagnall 0-4-0 industrial locomotive, and it was love at first sight. Pixie had been out of use for several years and birds had nested in the corners of her cab. Unfortunately at that time she was not for sale; however, after many months of negotiation and correspondence, she was pushed, on a rainy May day in 1962, on to a lorry deck heading for Cadeby.

Mr Boston recalls those early days and the excitement surrounding the advent of Pixie. Before her arrival, he says, 'back at the Rectory the working-parties had not been idle. A bill-hook was borrowed from the churchwarden and a path was made along the future line of the track. Work commenced, and the Rectory garden soon took on the appearance of a minor timber-yard. Loads of stone from the neighbouring Cliffe Hill quarry were delivered and this was carried in wheelbarrows to its position on the trackbed. Invaluable help came from the vicar of a neighbouring parish who claimed that his hobby was manual labour. In one afternoon we two clerics between us shifted over four tons of ballast.' Pixie has now trundled up and down this track some thousands of times carrying scores of visitors, and she even appears in the annual light-railway time-tables and guide.

As a young man studying at Cambridge, Teddy Boston ran the University Railway Club, having taken a lively interest in trains and engines for as long as he can remember. In the introduction to his own booklet, 'Rails Round the Rectory', he gives some of his thoughts on the subject:

The objects of the railway are simple. First, to provide an opportunity of seeing a steam locomotive at work without having to travel far from the centre of England. Second, to teach the railway 'staff' a little of what real railway work involves. There is more to be learnt, for example, about the permanent way by holding the business end of a sledge-hammer for ten minutes than by sitting in a comfortable chair reading track maintenance manuals for three hours! A third object is to produce a focus for steam interest in the shires and to keep this interest alive.

Many of the Rector's friends and neighbours were involved in the building of the track and he claims that it would not have been a possible project had he not had such firm support. One of his helpers was a former Lord Mayor of Leicester; Teddy Boston remembers that 'while we were re-packing a somewhat awkward valve gland on the 1903 steam roller, the ex-Lord Mayor, arms black to the elbows and with a happy smile on his face, turned to me and said, "Teddy, if anyone had told me thirty years ago when

Opposite: The Reverend Boston on board the Foster traction engine.

General view of station area. The model railway shed is on the left and the Foster traction engine on the right.

I had to work on these things for a living that I should one day be doing this for fun, I would have knocked his teeth in – but here we are!"'

The General Manager of the Cadeby Light Railway, the Rev. E. R. Boston, MA, has laid out a clear set of rules and regulations for the information of visitors:

1. At all times when the locomotive is moving under its own steam a 'passed driver' must be on the footplate.
2. When passengers are being carried, the brake on the guard's van must be manned by a qualified person.
3. 'Them as gets it off gets it on.'
4. 'Them as makes suggestions gets given the job.'

Since Pixie's first summer the track has been extended and various steam and 'infernal combustion' engines have crept into the Rectory garden. One of

Pixie's playmates is the 'Fiery Elias', an agricultural engine. She visits many rallies but when at home her steam is often raised on open days and she puffs up and down the drive making indentations for one of the rollers to flatten out again. Another, the Lilleshall Baguley Petrol Locomotive, at first proved extremely difficult to start and so was given the nickname of 'The Terror' – taken from Psalm 91, 'The terror that walketh in darkness', since it was always dark by the time the engine was actually going.

Among the diesels and traction engines in a shed bearing the legend 'Station Master's Office', Mr Boston houses his elaborate model railway. 'The object of this exercise,' he says, 'was to get a view of a railway working in a country landscape.' As his background he took a piece of South Devon, about

'Pixie' with Aveling and Porter steam roller resting at Cadeby locomotive shed.

six miles inland from Torquay, and put an imaginary junction on the Great Western line. The running of this miniature railway is a complicated enterprise, needing three signalmen and one driver on the main line alone. In order to have the system going at full blast a staff of ten is necessary. A speeded-up clock on the wall is set to go eight times as fast as a normal one, so that a day in the life of the railway lasts for three hours. Mr Boston operates his control panel to the blast of Handel organ concertos.

The walls of the shed are plastered with train timetables, and the model landscape (consisting of hills, tunnels, trees and buildings) is peppered with United Dairies milk tanks and toy railway props.

Beside the front door of the Rectory is a huge board saying 'London, Midland and Scottish Railway'. The inside of the house is decorated with paintings of trains and engines, copies of *Railway World*, labels, tickets and models. Railway ephemera are to be found in all corners – above the beds, across the piano and in the crowded library, which is also well stocked with books on railway history.

Enthusiasts come to Mr Boston with innumerable questions. As luck would have it his memory is good and he can often answer queries on the telephone without first having to look things up.

When the Cadeby Model Railway first came into being Teddy Boston was a bachelor. When he is asked how his wife, whom he married just over ten years ago, has taken to a train-filled Rectory and a steaming, flowerless garden, he replies, 'Well, she went into it with her eyes open!'

Architectural Relics

—CHARLES BROOKING—

Wooden sheds in the Brooking family garden explode with architectural fragments which, had they not been rescued from demolition sites, might well have been destroyed.

Door-knockers, sash windows, architraves and ironwork – all cleaned and chronicled – are in need of extra space if they are to be displayed as they deserve.

Recently the collection has generated interest on the part of architects and preservationists and the hope is that, before long, the Brooking Collection will be on permanent display in Central London.

Charles Brooking's awareness of shape and style started early. 'As a baby I was fascinated by the leather eyelets on the harness of my pram. Later, as I began to crawl, I became intrigued by a perspex ruler complete with magnifying glass. I was not much more than two when I started to notice various type-faces in bakelite gate-post numerals. My reaction was a yearning to possess them and from time to time I would gratify this longing, with the result that my mother had to organize replacements as tactfully as possible.'

Interest in form developed into an obsession. In 1958, at the age of four, Brooking became aware of door furniture and started to collect it. At this point the family moved to their present house near Guildford, which had been built in 1931. Wooden door-knobs fired his imagination and he was intrigued – just as a side-line – by terracotta air-bricks. Wooden mouldings, too, attracted his attention.

At this stage Charles Brooking's father was convinced that the hobby should be stamped out. He didn't like it at all and, although his mother was interested, Brooking's existence was a lonely one.

At the age of six he became aware of glazing-bars on windows, first taking an interest in the windows of his own family garage, which were being removed

Charles Brooking holding a carved pine Ionic capital from a doorcase of about 1785.

*The inside of a shed housing, amongst other things, a carved window
rescued from the Adelphi building in the Strand, mahogany doors from Waterloo Station (1920)
and window shutters from Nash Terrace, Regent's Park, c. 1822–5.*

*Opposite: Part of an 1840s fanlight, a selection of 1850–80 foot-scrapers
and a small oval cast-iron window from the Cutler Street Warehouses, London.*

as their frames had rotted. Having examined the mouldings on these windows he cut sections and took them out. Soon he discovered that many of the Victorian houses in and around Guildford had double-hung sashes which were complicated and had interesting mouldings.

This was the beginning of an obsession which nearly drove his father mad. Brooking was too young to go on to sites then; he could only seize the opportunities offered by shopping trips, when he looked for small bits of tile or anything with an exciting shape.

In the *Children's Encyclopaedia* of 1960 he saw an illustration of a complete sash window and yearned to possess one: mechanism, pulleys and weights. A teacher at the first school he attended said, 'You can't have one of those. They're dangerous. You shouldn't be interested in that sort of thing. You should take an interest in nature and fishing.' His teachers were of the opinion that his obsession with architectural fragments interfered with his school work; only lately has Charles Brooking discovered that he has always been dyslexic.

In order to acquire a complete sash window Brooking had to visit demolition sites in Guildford; for this he had to rely on his father, who was not only very strict but was opposed to the venture. A bargain had to be struck. Mr Brooking believed that Sunday should be a day of rest and thought that all activities on that day should be devoted to religion. There was to be no playing in the garden; no lighting of bonfires. Brooking worked it out and consented to attend church service without a fuss if his father, as his part of the agreement, would take him to demolition sites. Unfortunately these site visits were allowed to last for only five minutes and the workmen always said that the windows were too difficult to take out in so short a space of time. Eventually a builder uncle was able to acquire one for his nephew, and there he was – at last – with a working example. From then on Brooking made a study of sash windows: dating, chronicling and recording in great detail. This first window formed the basis of an unrivalled collection. Brooking considers the sash window to be extremely important in the conservation sense since many are being incorrectly replaced in Georgian buildings and his own collection provides a useful reference.

The acquisition of the sash window led to greater things, but when Brooking left his first school, his father put his foot down, saying, 'I'm not helping with this venture any more. You've got to get on and think about other things.' He encouraged his son to take an interest in fossils. Brooking hated games and would play truant from school in order to search for fossils and stone-age implements. It was fun, but his thoughts always returned to architecture, building construction, and materials.

In 1966, at the age of twelve, he decided to take up his old interest once again, and with renewed enthusiasm he was soon immersed in the complete history of door-knockers, door furniture and fireplaces. In 1968, on his fourteenth birthday, he was given his first shed; his parents had at last realized that the dedication was likely to last. From then on the collection grew, and he specialized in windows, doors and staircases.

Charles Brooking left school not knowing exactly what he was going to do, but owning a vast accumulation of fittings, decorative tiles, fireplaces and fanlights. He took a job in the architectural department of British Rail, but it wasn't closely enough related to his own particular passion. He worried about his future, yet continued to rescue things: a tricky business, as he has never been able to drive a car. He was obliged to carry heavy objects around or hire people to pick them up. After moving from job to job he found, only a few years ago, a local architect who employs and sponsors him.

Although Brooking now has several sheds, they are crowded out, and the space is too small for further outbuildings. He wants to find somewhere large enough to house his all-embracing collection. There are already museums whose displays incorporate architectural detail, but none that cover the subject in any great depth.

Brooking's dream is of 'the creation of a permanent collection and associated library covering important architectural details of the period 1700 to 1930, for the specific use of architects and those involved in the preservation of buildings of this period'. The intention is that it should be used for reference – 'not just a back-yard crank's collection'. He hopes that it will be set up as a trust and will provide a complete service for those involved in restoration. At the moment it is all a bit uncertain, but conservationists have heard

A very small part of Charles Brooking's large collection of window and door furniture.

about Charles Brooking and consider the venture to be more than worth while.

Meanwhile in the Guildford garden, almost unviewable through lack of space, are windows from the Ritz Hotel, sections of the old Swan and Edgar store and a fireplace from Elizabeth Barrett Browning's bedroom. Brooking is always being tipped off but finds it hard to keep up with the chase. It can be dismaying to arrive late and find that an important piece has already been removed. Brooking is a man with a mission, recognizing that much of the past is in great danger of being obliterated, and that without his efforts fragments of history will inevitably be lost.

At the age of thirty-one he has come a long way in his quest. Although in his teens he rebelled in his own way by refusing to submit to convention, he didn't lose time. Even now, he hates Bank Holidays as they slow things up. Acutely aware of the tragedy of the passing of time, he would like to have been granted at least two hundred years in which to achieve his ambitions, 'not just a measly seventy or eighty'.

Angler's Equipment

—RAY CANNON—

Ray Cannon has collected everything to do with angling for over thirty years. When he started, 'it was good fun. While most lads went for stamps and cigarette-cards, I preferred to spend my paper-round money on two-shilling brass reels.' Cannon began fishing at the age of seven, when his foster-father taught him the basics. He became deeply involved, explaining that 'if you take a lad to the river bank and he sits there for three hours and catches nothing, that's not good enough; but if something wiggles on the end of the line then he will probably be hooked for life. Luck comes into it, but any teacher should

insist on taking a beginner to the right place; somewhere you can be sure he'll catch something that will get him going.'

From his early start with wooden and brass reels, Cannon carried on and built up an enormous collection which now comprises something like 4,000 items. As he collected he became inquisitive and had to find out who made what, what sort of character the craftsman might have been and where the various things came from.

Cannon feels that his collection has become a part of the country's heritage and should remain here. He

Above: A group of fly wallets and containers. There are wet and dry flies and, at the bottom, salmon flies.

believes that it deserves to have its own museum, since none exists in England, and the subject covers not only fishing but engineering, manufacture and design. He explains that 'it doesn't just involve the little fisherman. It involves about every hobby there is. Stamps, coins (fishing-tackle makers and fish-markets produced their own stamps and token coinage) and postcards on the subject of angling.'

Lately Cannon set up an angling exhibition in the Guildhall at Winchester, where taped bird music trilled from trees beside a river and waterfall, and fish grew from four to fifteen inches in a three-month period. Most of his own material – including pieces used to teach apprentice engineers how to file and shape during the Industrial Revolution, a human-bone hook found in the Peruvian foothills, and bound goose quills with ivory tops – formed part of the display. Cannon hopes, eventually, to write a book on angler's equipment but is beginning to doubt whether he is capable of covering such an enormously wide field.

He spends much of his spare time sea-fishing on local beaches and deep-sea-fishing from marinas and boats, but he still finds time for a great deal of fly-fishing. He also teaches fly-dressing and casting twice a week at night school.

Ray Cannon's reels, flies, rods and baits are in wonderful condition. This, in his view, is partly because most people who fish buy far more equipment than they ever use – 'all sorts of fancy gadgets that look good in the shop. Everybody who takes up a hobby tends to acquire mountains of unnecessary stuff.'

The first piece that Cannon ever owned was given to him when he was nine. It was an old brass reel with a silk line. The Scotsman who gave it to him said that when young Cannon had cleaned it up he would take him to the water and show him how to cast a fly. 'That he did, and I remember every little detail of the day. That first brass reel really started it. I'm a bit like a magpie. I've never sold a fishing item although I will let objects out on hire to stage and cinema productions.'

Cannon does an enormous amount of charity work, usually setting up a marquee at country fairs where he demonstrates and encourages the public to take part. There are said to be about four million anglers in Britain of which about a million are fly-

Various items of angling memorabilia, including nets, gaffs, bait containers, lines, scales, retrieving rings and trace holders.

fishermen, many of them fanatics. Cannon owns that 'there may be as many people playing darts and pool, but those things come and go as crazes whereas angling continues'.

Ray Cannon is certain that his hobby would be destroyed if he were to use it for his livelihood and that his angling might peter out. It has gone beyond being a collection; with the help of libraries and history books, he has solved many hundreds of identification problems. Indian shell hooks from North America, Victorian bait-cans, white horsehair lines, and reels of aluminium, brass and ebonite – all have been researched, and carefully labelled and classified.

Neither Ray Cannon's wife nor any of his four daughters takes the slightest interest in fishing or in its equipment. They, in making their own collections, cast their lines in other waters.

Museum of Curiosity and Other Antiquities
—JAMES CARTLAND—

Harley House, Arundel, with its owner's 1932 Rolls-Royce standing before it, gives the impression of long and unbroken ownership. It could well have been handed from father to son for over two centuries without alteration or embellishment, apart from the addition of Victorian clutter. It is barely possible to believe, though it happens to be true, that James Cartland, his many cats and his thousands of possessions have been settled there for less than five years.

Cartland is a collector of antiques *par excellence*, collecting collections within collections. Many of these tie in with one another: for example, a large number of glass salt-cellars of some rarity, each

showing the likeness of a member of the Court of King George III and at present stowed away in a drawer, relate to some of the hundreds of portrait silhouettes that cover the walls.

Cartland describes himself as a 'manic collector' and lives in a haze of hair from Napoleon's horse, Doctor Johnson's writing-case, his own great-aunt's dolls, parasols, the preserved foetus of a chihuahua, packs of miniature playing-cards, buildings modelled in cork and shells, glass ships, and a bit of lace once the property of Queen Elizabeth I: all this in addition to a fine collection of antique furniture. The basement kitchen of Harley House jangles with

Opposite: James Cartland with his cat in a corner of his dining room.

*Above: A drawerful of rare glass salt-cellars,
each showing the likeness of a member of the court of King George III.*

Treasures, including a turret-shaped ink-well,
a lock of Edward IV's hair (removed from his coffin) and a silver rattle.

mugs, an ancient mangle and a vast round knife-sharpener. There is also an instrument called a 'serpent' from a church band, and an old black anthracite cooker.

In the front hall of Harley House a fifteenth-century misericorde, once used by monks to rest on during church services, hangs above the door. A multiple hook, bought in a Turkish bazaar, is suspended by a window, 'for hanging vegetables on, or dead cats or whatever'.

Once, James Cartland says, he sneezed and a lock of Edward IV's hair flew around the room; cats walk over bundles of Prince Albert's letters and other treasures. Cartland sorrows over the 'craze for excessive cleaning – it's a recent thing. There must be something wrong with the human race.'

Cartland started to collect at the age of six, and he admits that 'some people call me insane'. By the time he was ten he had enough stuff with which to set up a small museum. At school he used to swap sweets for curios, and now his objects and his way of life are inextricably entwined.

Harley House is open to the public on request. Cartland says that 'the collecting thing just sort of evolved; looking back, it's extraordinary. I left school when I was sixteen. I've always been a bit of a loner, and hated being told what to do and what not to do.'

After leaving school he took a job in an antique shop where he met a man named Irving who collected pipes. Irving asked Cartland if he would help him sell not only his pipes but Potter's Museum of Curiosity in Arundel, an extraordinary collection of taxidermy which he also owned. Cartland ended up by keeping the museum, which he runs, tends and embellishes. Although he does still deal, there is absolutely nothing in his house that is for sale. Sometimes, for reasons of space or economy, he will get rid of one thing in order to buy something else, but only if it's a question of making an improvement.

James Cartland is now thirty-eight, but was asked the other day by an anxious friend, 'What on earth are you going to be like when you're seventy?' Cartland explains that some of his friends are wary of clutter – 'I think they're frightened of being included in my will and of having to sort through all this stuff.'

Of an evening James Cartland comes back to his typical eighteenth-century merchant's house where he feels that he's enveloped in another era, distancing himself from modern habits which he doesn't like at all'.

Now Cartland would really like a small country house and more involvement with architecture and preservation, but he thinks that it might be too much of an undertaking on his own. He had planned to do this when he was married but, sadly, his wife has taken her leave.

He imagines that the need to acquire makes up for something else; that objects provide the type of company that can't answer back. He also thinks that excessive collecting is a very English characteristic: 'maybe it is to do with our situation in the world; we've never been conquered and so many collections have been built up – giving us something to aim for.'

One of the pleasures, for Cartland, in collecting is the forging of links with other people. Both his house and his museum court interesting people: screw-makers, or the world's greatest living expert on match-boxes. 'I'll let the electricity bill go by the board if I see something that I must have. Half the fun is in the chase and things can turn a bit dead when they come home. I don't look for things. I just see and want them.'

James Cartland was adopted at an early age and he is absolutely sure that he collects in order to provide himself with roots. For the same reason he has always been interested in family trees. He likes things to look as though they'd been there for ever. He knows a great deal about people who are dead but often he can't remember the names of people he knows – he has even, on a few occasions, forgotten his own name (particularly when answering the telephone). When he's dead he thinks that he'll probably remember it.

Cartland wanders through a vast aggregate of curling-tongs, appliqué bedspreads, Egyptian masks, gas-lamps, miniatures, teapots galore, stuffed birds, ivories, ancient bathroom scales and Elizabeth Barrett Browning's father's watch. These wonders muddle in with Mayan pottery and panels of stained glass. In the dining-room lives a stuffed hen; it is called Duplicate and, as the world egg-laying champion, is reputed to have laid four hundred and sixty-two eggs in less than two years. Duplicate has her own scrapbook and boasts an obituary in *The Times*.

Fingering a pair of ear-rings shaped as penises and rescued from Pompeii, Cartland sighs over the fact that, thanks to the big auction houses, antiques have become items of value in which people invest, so making it nearly impossible for children to collect in the way he did himself.

It would certainly not be easy for dealers to settle on prices for the contents of the Museum of Curiosity. How do you value a stuffed-kittens' tea-party, a pig with six legs, snakes in bottles or a mummified hand?

A Collection
from China and Japan
— SIR CHRISTOPHER CHANCELLOR —

It may come as a surprise to those visiting Sir Christopher and Lady Chancellor's medieval priory in east Somerset to find that the interior is, for the most part, hung with paintings from China and Japan.

Christopher Chancellor was twenty-seven when he was appointed Reuter's General Manager in the Far East. In 1931 he travelled to China by train on the Trans-Siberian Railway. A month after his arrival in Shanghai, which was to be his home for eight years, a Japanese army invaded Manchuria and a division of Japanese troops landed at Shanghai. War between China and Japan continued until 1939 when Sir Christopher and his family were ordered home and were fortunate to escape before the Second World War broke out.

During his period in the Far East Christopher Chancellor was almost always travelling. Shanghai was his base, but he had to keep in touch with Reuter's offices in China, Japan, Hong Kong and Manila. When he was on his extensive travels he built up his collection of Chinese and Japanese pictures as well as a vast number of miscellaneous pieces of porcelain. When a picture or some other *objet d'art* caught his eye in a remote antique shop in Peking or Tokyo, he would buy it and bring it back to Shanghai.

Some of these purchases were eccentric and the collection came to be a strange mixture. He and his wife were delighted with it and their favourite hunting-grounds were shops that produced pictures with some European connection. They concentrated on paintings by Chinese artists between the beginning of the eighteenth and the middle of the nineteenth century. By this time China and Japan had opened their gates to Europe and the rest of the civilized world after hundreds of years of isolation. They had

a strong interest in Chinese 'foreign pictures', painted by Chinese artists and depicting Europe and Europeans. In this they were assisted by copies and prints of European pictures brought to Peking by foreign embassies. Chancellor was also interested in export pictures painted on glass – scenes of China and portraits of imaginary Europeans.

Christopher Chancellor did not regard himself as a serious collector in those days and took little interest in the early dynasties, although tourists who came to Peking, mostly from America, used to buy ancient scrolls – for the full enjoyment of which it is necessary to be able to understand Chinese calligraphy and to have a scholar's knowledge of Chinese poetry and philosophy.

Apart from one important exception, Chancellor never met anyone in Peking who was interested in the same type of picture as he was. The exception was an old friend, Sir Harold Acton, who had been at school with him and had arrived in China at the same time. Acton went north to live in Peking and, once he had settled in his exotic house there, Chancellor used to stay with him when he visited Reuter's Peking office.

On these occasions Acton arranged for groups of antique-dealers to come to his house after breakfast to show what 'Chinese foreign pictures' they had for sale. Chancellor took his purchases back to Shanghai to ensure their safety. A few years later there came a sad disaster when, in 1937, a Japanese army occupied, looted and destroyed Acton's house in Peking, together with everything in it.

At the beginning of the eighteenth century a formidable mission of Jesuit fathers arrived in Peking from Rome for the purpose of persuading the Chinese emperor and his mandarins to accept

Opposite: Christopher Chancellor with a portrait of the Fragrant Concubine by Father Castiglione,
a T'ang horse and Foo-Chow blanc-de-chine Chinese figures in the drawing room.

Above: An eighteenth-century English bureau bookcase (almost certainly sent to China to be lacquered) displaying Cantonese enamel bowls and nineteenth-century Chinese figures.

Opposite: A nineteenth-century 'ancestory' portrait bought in Peking, an eighteenth-century painting of rice fields and Imari bowls in a corner of the library.

· 49 ·

Christianity as China's official religion. These missionaries, a group of brilliant men, had been chosen for their scholarship. When they arrived in Peking they were welcomed warmly by Ch'ing Lung, China's greatest emperor, who was particularly impressed by two members of the mission, both distinguished artists. An Italian, Giuseppe Castiglione, was the emperor's favourite. He was given many privileges, and his Chinese name, Lang Shih Ming, was widely known and shown on all his pictures. He could converse and write in Chinese and attired himself as a mandarin at the palace. Ch'ing Lung and Lang Shih Ming became close friends and in the collection at Ditcheat Priory there is a portrait on silk signed with their joint seals. Chancellor bought it from a dealer in Peking, and it has always been believed to be a portrait of the famous Mohammedan princess who was brought back as a prisoner to Peking by the Chinese emperor after a successful war against Chinese Turkestan in 1741. Castiglione enjoyed painting this beautiful princess in European clothes, and in the picture she is dressed as a French shepherdess of the period and is known as Hsiang Fei, 'the Fragrant Concubine'.

Castiglione was born in Italy in 1668 and died in Peking in 1766. He made a gallant effort to persuade his friend the emperor that it would be good for China to become a Roman Catholic country. Here he failed. The Chinese were matter-of-fact on the subject of religion and wished to know what advantages there would be for them; would it be worth while? Ch'ing Lung himself asked Castiglione in what way Europe could be helpful to China. As an example, Castiglione put forward the fact that in China there was only one breed of dog whereas in Europe there were twenty-five breeds. The emperor ordered Castiglione to go out and paint him one. A huge and colourful painting of a hunting dog, now hanging in Sir Christopher's library, was the skilful result of this fruitless effort to convert China.

In the library, too, a large picture of rice-fields outside Peking is sealed with Castiglione's characters and is an interesting example of the then recently discovered use of perspective in Chinese painting. Fields and trees stretch away in Western style, but Chinese faces and buildings confirm its origin. Before Castiglione's arrival in Peking the Chinese had no knowledge of the laws of perspective. Their paintings were flat, without depth, distance or shadow, and he brought about a revolution in their technique.

Castiglione was a forerunner of the British painter Chinnery, who later taught his pupils in Macao and Hong Kong to paint in oils in the European style. Of these, too, Sir Christopher Chancellor has some striking examples.

Beneath the portrait of the Fragrant Concubine there prances a dark red horse, one of a pair, with a waving tail and mane. Chancellor bought this in Hankow just as the Japanese invaded. He was there as the guest of the British Ambassador, who took one of the pair while Chancellor took the other. Many years later one of the horses, presumably at some stage sold by the Ambassador, was shown in the pages of Country Life. Later still, this horse's new owner, an American lady, came by chance to Sir Christopher's house in Somerset and said, 'There's the pair to my horse! I must have it.' Since then she has written many times offering tantalizing sums, but Sir Christopher always says 'No'.

Many of the floors of the house are covered in faded Kansu rugs of pale yellow and pink. They used to come by camel from Turkestan to Peking, where they were spread out on the pavements to be bought by dealers.

The old, dark Priory is brilliantly brought to life by animated horses (which cannot be dated precisely unless they are broken), bowls of Chinese porcelain fruit and blue-and-white ovoid jardinières painted with fantastic and fiery dragons.

Unicorns

—LADY DIANA COOPER—

As a promise of things to come, an iron unicorn crouches on all fours in the front garden of Lady Diana Cooper's house overlooking the canal at Paddington.

On the drawing-room mantelpiece a white-painted unicorn rears up, sporting a banner and protected by a glass case. Nearby, on a velvet-covered table, stands a tiny china one, missing his horn; then a prancing one, on a gold plinth which stands on a marble-topped table in a corner of the room. In the hall, half-hidden under the stairway, a huge head of one of these mythical beasts is mounted.

It is in the owner's bedroom (where, to use her own words, she 'weightless lies' upon a white cano-pied bed beside a parchment-coloured lamp, the shade of which is boldly stamped with the print of a unicorn) that the chief treasures are stored.

Everybody has known for so long that Lady Diana collects unicorns that people only have to see one in order to present her with it. She held up a gold brooch – unicorn-shaped. It goes from hat to hat; she pins it on to whichever one she intends to wear.

Clasping her diminutive dog, Diana Cooper told me that 'there is a comic lady who lives near Taunton and has a complex of chihuahuas – like Doggy. She has six of them and when I go abroad Doggy stays with her. She provides me with unicorns. She made that.' She points to an embroidered cushion on the sofa. Doggy's bowl has a lively unicorn on its base.

Above: Prints, drawings and unicorn ornaments in the bathroom.

Lady Diana, reflected in the glass, with a selection of unicorns on a unicorn-patterned tablecloth.

'Why unicorns?' I asked. Chuckling, she touched the centre of her forehead. 'I've got a bump here. No, you wouldn't see it, but it's there.'

She looked to the wall where, beside the mirror, hangs a watercolour painting of a dancing unicorn. 'That one I like,' she said. 'I like it very much.'

On a table by the bed and beneath the lamp is a wax candle in the form of a unicorn, and a copper cigarette-lighter, much used, with one stamped on its side – 'Artemis, my granddaughter, found it in a market.'

She handed me a 'magic' one. I held a transparent disc in my hand and slowly a single-horned form came into focus. Diana Cooper, with a throaty laugh, said, 'It's called a halibut or something.'

We looked at blue-and-gold tiles decorated with unicorns while their owner told me, 'There are a great many theories about them and the main one is that they are entirely imaginary and never did exist. I do believe in them. Unicorns were the size of goats. Quite small. The brontosaurus was so big that it lasted; its bones were easy to collect. Unicorns were too small to stand the test of time, but I don't see why they shouldn't have existed. No point, really, in inventing them.'

She went on to say that, although usually ferocious, unicorns could always be tamed by the beauty of a virgin. The virgin would attract the beast to her by means of a mirror, after which he would follow her meekly and nestle his head on her lap. This theory was seconded by W. H. Auden in a verse from 'The Quest', which Diana Cooper's son, John Julius Norwich, included for his mother's delight in his commonplace book – the *Christmas Cracker* of 1971:

> They noticed that virginity was needed
> To trap the unicorn in every case,
> But not that, of those virgins who succeeded,
> A high percentage had an ugly face.

'Somebody once sent me a postcard of the Duke of Norfolk's coat-of-arms,' said Lady Diana. 'They were just the same as the royal arms except that, instead of lions, there were two unicorns. Neither of them had horns. I wrote to the head man and asked, "Why don't your unicorns have horns? They're obviously unicorns. Everything about them is unicorn. Narrow tails with tassels on the end." He wrote back, rather sharply, and said that they weren't unicorns at all.

That they were horses. "All right," I said. Then on another occasion he wrote again and said, "I've already told you. They're horses" – but their tails gave them away.'

Lots of people write to Lady Diana on the subject of unicorns: 'Any amount. They write about unicorns and about everything. I answer them if there's a question or something.' In her time Diana Cooper has received stacks and stacks of postcards. 'People see a postcard with a unicorn on it and they send it to me.'

She lay back on her pillows; very slowly, and with perfect enunciation, she quoted from her favourite nursery-rhyme:

> The lion and the unicorn were fighting for the crown,
> The lion chased the unicorn all around the town.
> Some gave them white bread and some gave them brown,
> Some gave them plum cake and chased them out of town.

I asked her if there were any good books about unicorns. 'Not that I've read. No. I don't think that there are. People aren't very interested in them.'

Before leaving I stumbled on another bevy of the beasts, half-hidden by a curtain on the window-sill – a weird glass one made in Venice especially commissioned for her by the painter Lawrence Mynott, and next to this a merry-go-round of plastic unicorns: green, yellow, pink and purple. I asked about it, and Lady Diana replied, 'That one just happened.' Beside this happening stood a tall-stemmed engraved glass given to her by Edward Fox and a handsome pink box with a unicorn set in relief on the lid. That one was new, a present from a friend. 'He's a friend I've had for forty years, I suppose. I've known him since middle age. We became attached to each other when I was Ambassadress in Paris and he was a very rich man. He's very good about everything. As well as unicorns he sends me, always, a soothing sleep drug. I can't remember what it's called.'

I peered past the window-sill to the garden below where once lived a pair of identical stone unicorns. They were given to Lady Diana by her friend Garrett Drogheda. Alas, they were stolen; although beastly of the burglar, this was rather ingenious as they were both extremely heavy and, although they were known as Siamese unicorns, one went a week or two before the other. Following the theft there was a heart-rending piece in *The Times* lamenting their loss.

Prams, Mail Carts and Bassinets

—JACK HAMPSHIRE—

Jack Hampshire quite understandably supposes himself to be one of the few men in the world to have ten prams in his bedroom, but in this room dolls are not allowed to occupy them. 'They would watch me undressing and that would give me a nasty feeling.'

It is not only the bedroom (where the floor slopes, occasioning the odd unexpected journey) that is overrun with hoods and wheels. The whole of Hampshire's moated manor house near Maidstone (including two Queen Anne oast-houses attached to the property) is stuffed with over four hundred perambulators representing every year since the beginning of the century and earlier; each one has its own particular history, and there is room for little else in the way of furniture. He has carved out a corner for himself in the bedroom, and it is in this

room that, for the most part, he lives. Dusty prams crowd the sitting-room, the dining-room and even the lavatory.

In the introduction to his own book, *Prams, Mail Carts and Bassinets*, Hampshire tells us that there are many museums where one can see and admire the old horse-drawn carriages, vintage motor-cars, steam locomotives and most other forms of transport. 'But where,' he asks, 'may one go to see a complete collection of prams? By complete I mean several hundred, for that's the very minimum I would consider necessary to show properly their history and development.'

Jack Hampshire describes himself as a conservationist first and foremost, and abhors the thoughtless destruction of so much of our past. His collection

Opposite: Hampshire with prams in the drawing room.

Above: More prams and dolls in a semi-outhouse.

Part of Jack Hampshire's Kent bedroom.

Opposite: A regiment of prams leading to the nearby oast-houses.

(which dates from the earliest known examples of babies' prams, some made of metal, some incorporating chip-carved wood and reedwork, with twin, folding and every other sort of specimen) manifests his determination to make a contribution towards conserving our heritage. 'Today,' he says, 'we rush too readily to arms. We're caught up in the love of tanks and guns. People don't like gentle things like prams any more.'

He considers himself to be an eccentric and has his 'own queer way' of doing things. 'What I like about prams is the early memories they provoke. In your youngest days you have time to think. As you get older it's quite surprising the thoughts that flood back.' He remembers lying in his pram in the garden and watching biplanes flying overhead. These memories are becoming more and more vivid to him. He thinks, too, that the perambulating method was a delightful and unhurried one. 'Nowadays you see mothers shoving their babies into a supermarket trolley and then rushing out and throwing them into the back of a car. Lots of the people who come here actually want to lie in a pram. It takes them back.'

Many famous people formed their first thoughts under canopies now installed in the Kent manor house, but according to Hampshire they are sometimes reluctant to have that fact disclosed. They do, however, trace and visit their old prams, often bringing their own children with them. This can lead to complications, particularly when they want to pop the child into the appropriate receptacle, often causing rage and embarrassment.

Prams on the upper landing are mostly occupied by teddy-bears, which sit bolt upright tucked in under antique covers beside an 1870 'wheeled beauty' that stands in a place of honour at the top of the ancient stairs.

Apart from the mice that tend to nestle in many of the prams, Hampshire's main worry lies in wondering what will happen to his collection when he's dead. His children aren't interested; in fact they are embarrassed by their father's pram-dominated ménage. Both his boys, 'who are very masculine and have lots of girl friends', think that his interest is 'perverted'.

Jack Hampshire campaigns for his collection to be turned into a museum, but he is not finding the task an easy one. 'Bloody civil servants. How I hate them.

I had a letter from one the other day concerning prams and it made me absolutely livid.'

The pram collection came into existence by pure chance. 'I think that most of life is made up of chance. Things just happen to you.' It took Jack Hampshire fifteen years to amass his collection, but then, he says, 'I'm not a civil servant. I work very fast. When you're self-employed you work harder and faster than the rest.' His active interest in it started about twenty years ago when his late wife Vicki persuaded him to bid for a toy pram at a local auction. It was this pram that led him to research the much-neglected subject. From then on he and his wife decided to save the disappearing pram. 'You don't find things like these in Regent's Park any more. The Queen has four and most of the landed gentry keep one or two on their country estates but, by and large, they've disappeared. They've been replaced by absolute abortions – no other name for the things that people will put their children into nowadays. I'm old-fashioned. That's the reason that I live in an old-fashioned house. I don't like modern things at all.'

Hampshire has seen two world wars and, having been very active in the last one, is now an ardent pacifist. He has come to the conclusion that 'it's no use beating the old chap over the head; the best thing to do is to have a shake and talk the whole thing over'.

When his own children were small he didn't push them around in their prams. He told his wife that it was beneath his dignity – although occasionally he would man the big carriage-pram. He believes that the old-fashioned pram will come back into fashion. 'In a few years' time, if the atom bomb hasn't got us, people will want to go back to a quieter way of life. Today you see so many strained faces peering out of the windows of motor-cars.'

Since the tragic death of his much-loved wife Vicki (to whom he was married for thirty-four years and from whom he never spent a day apart), shortly before the completion of his book ('which took ten years of bloody hard work'), Hampshire has lived alone with his prams, with acres of cobwebs and with an ancient, arthritic cat. He is firm that nothing should ever be sprayed with woodworm-killer: 'When Vicki and I first came here the place was full of bats. We treated the beams with the stuff. It was stupid of us. Now there isn't a bat left. Very sad.'

Wemyss Ware

—DEREK HILL—

Derek Hill, the artist, has left various pieces of his Wemyss Ware collection in Ireland. These, with his house and other treasures, he has given to the Irish government. He has, however, always kept some examples of the pottery in England which is where he started to collect it, having done so since his early adult life as a reminder of Nanny and the nursery and the jam-pots and honeycomb dishes on the breakfast table. These 'English' ones, stored in the house of a friend, are the ones shown here.

Derek Hill's adult taste for Wemyss was entirely nostalgic and it never occurred to him that the brightly coloured pottery would ever come to have much value. In the introductory passage to a Wemyss Ware exhibition catalogue of 1976 Derek Hill explained his early interest:

Breakfast in the nursery and the first memories of Wemyss Ware. 'Little' Nanny presiding – so small she sometimes failed to control my enormous Millsom pram as it hurtled down a hill; but when she left I stood in her trunk in a vain attempt to stop the inevitable packing, tears streaming down my face. With her departure came the first experience of desirable life not continuing; the first realization that nothing was permanent. With Nanny the Wemyss Ware seemed to disappear too, and a series of detested governesses whisked away or broke the jam-pots, honeycomb dishes and egg-cups I had loved. The excitement one day when a blackberry jam-pot had arrived with stalk and leaves as a handle on top! Now all that was left was the black 'cock and hen' set with 'Bonjour' on it as a reminder that it was high time to start lessons. The 'Bonjour' somehow became part of my father's determination to get me out of bed: 'Get up, Monsieur le Comte. You have great things to do today.' A motto over the bed would shake when the wall was banged and 'Get up Maggot' was yelled at me from his dressing-room next door.

It was not until many years later that the determination to recapture the delights of the pre-governess nursery world made me begin to collect Wemyss Ware and to pick up pieces that I feel must have been smashed when 'little'

Above: A 'chimney' vase c.1880–90, painted with a cock and a bee by Karel Nekola.

Nanny left. How far sentimental nostalgia has heightened my appreciation I cannot decide. The late 'jazz'-type ware and figurative pieces such as Toby Jugs and Fair Maids of Perth do not, to my mind, have the artistic merit of those painted by Karel Nekola. Pigs, large or small, appeal only as notes of colour in the decorative scheme of a room. In general, in my view, all Wemyss Ware goes best on mahogany or dark wood. Some pieces by Nekola are exquisite – the great butter pans with eight-inch rims painted with purple and green grapes or vine leaves; vases and garden seats with foxgloves, roses or corn. The fuchsia sets are especially desirable, and the bedroom ware patterned with wild ducks and reeds. More quaint are the three-monkey groups – 'hear no evil, see no evil, speak no evil' – and the Earlshall sets with black crows, black trees, and perhaps only a brown rabbit to enliven the lonely scene.

Most successful, I feel sure, are the pieces inspired by flowers or fruit and luckily there seems to be an almost unending number of these. Hitherto unknown patterns constantly appear. A nasturtium vase found in a junk-shop, a pansy mug, a gorse hat-pin holder; rarer still, in the bird world, a slop-pail with pink flamingoes painted on it, and a set of birds of prey plates signed by Nekola himself. All these snatches of news that come to the collector's ear add excitement and stimulation, even if they represent a dire blot on the account book. In the fever of catching up with the new discoveries the dear old nursery favourites tend to be forgotten: the cherries and apples, plums and roses of the breakfast or night-nursery set. The awful moment when Miss Benn, most disliked of all governesses, broke the clover-painted potty, in which she hid her illicit cigarette ends, as she clumsily pulled it out from under my bed. Perhaps it was her hatred of the nursery ware, which still represents to me the glorious nursery era, that has made my liking of it so acute today; that has helped me to see through rose-coloured spectacles a make of pottery that I might otherwise have neglected.

In the history of Wemyss Ware the great inspiration, of whom Hill writes, was Karel Nekola. He is said to have come to East Fife in about 1880, with other artists from Bohemia; there he was appointed decorator to the existing Fife pottery. Tentative steps had already been taken in the development of this ware and some of the commoner motifs such as roses, apples and cherries were already being painted in a stiff manner, far removed from the free-flowering of the later style of Wemyss.

Fife must have proved forbidding to artists in exile because, with only one exception, they soon returned to the Continent. Karel Nekola was the excep-

tion and he remained to become chief decorator at the pottery and to train local artists to work as his assistants. Under his care the pottery flourished and became immensely successful. Greatly assisted by the patronage of local lairds, Wemyss (the name was taken from nearby Wemyss Castle) became a much sought-after product. Before long it was discovered by Thomas Goode and Company of Mayfair, and Goode became the sole retail outlet in England. Country-house owners flocked to buy bedroom, bathroom, nursery and servants' hall sets: slop-pails, jugs and bowls, soap-dishes and candle-holders.

Nekola had the reputation of being fiery and bad-tempered but, despite working under tremendous pressure, he brought the pottery into high repute; he eventually married a local girl and settled to raise a family in Scotland. He died at the age of fifty-eight, having spent thirty years in Fife. In 1916 Edwin Sandland took over as director and new designs were introduced. By 1928 Sandland had died and the end was in sight. After ups and downs the sole agency passed into the hands of a Czech, Jan Plichta, and under his name a popular series of animals was produced, decorated with clover, roses and other flowers. Joseph Nekola, son of Karel, worked with Plichta and it was on his death in 1952 that the famous pottery finally died out.

When Derek Hill started to collect, Wemyss Ware pieces were very cheap indeed. Now, of course, they are regarded as antiques and people will happily pay large sums for them. Derek Hill did inherit one or two of the cracked jam-pots from his own nursery but, apart from these, his earliest acquisition is a ravishing and unusual inkwell given to him by Lady Victoria Wemyss, who lived at Wemyss Castle and said, handing it to him, 'Hate the stuff.' At that point it was still considered shabby servants'-hall rubbish. Derek Hill's array of campanula-covered cream jugs, glistening fruit-covered vases, designs of honeysuckle and bees, dancing hares and thistle-patterned candle-sticks are a fitting memorial to 'little' Nanny, and it is hard to believe that this highly glazed and brilliantly coloured pottery could ever have been despised.

As well as its nostalgic value, the lure of Wemyss Ware lies in its rarity. It is very brittle because it was fired at low temperatures in order to produce a soft 'biscuit' body to absorb colours from a paintbrush.

Derek Hill holding a vase painted by Karel Nekola with mixed flowers, including roses and fox-gloves, c. 1890.

Derek Hill laments having missed the Wemyss copy of a Chinese garden seat. The price at the time seemed phenomenal but now . . .

Derek Hill is partly responsible for Wemyss having become the cult it is today. Once in his early collecting days he unfortunately mentioned it to a Scottish friend, asking him if, on his behalf, he'd keep a look-out for Wemyss Ware. Before long his friend had amassed a far larger collection than Hill's own. Collectors cannot be too cautious.

In its time Scotland has been the most fertile hunting-ground. In Perth, Derek Hill found an extra-ordinary umbrella-stand given by Karel Nekola as a present to his daughters. It was simply a common drainpipe that Nekola had painted with huge cabbage-roses, having first constructed a heavy pottery base.

Derek Hill doesn't buy much Wemyss Ware any more – 'too expensive' – but, were he to stumble on a rare piece decorated with flamingoes, gooseberries or holly (holly in particular), he might succumb. He does have one gooseberry jam-pot lid but nothing more; perhaps one day he'll find a complete pot under a gooseberry bush.

Milk Bottles

—*MIKE & NAOMI HULL*—

According to the author of an article in the first edition of the *Milk Bottle News*, the collecting of British milk bottles has now become respectable. He goes on to say that credit for this must lie with the recent burst of advertising that has transformed the milk bottle from an ordinary container into an object of interest.

Through a milk-bottle article Mike Hull corresponded with a lady from Ayrshire, Margaret Barber, and the magazine was founded in 1984. Hull and Barber take it in turns to do the editorial work, and they enjoy it. The idea of the magazine is to put various groups in touch for swapping and sleuthing. Several of the fifty subscribers have been in the dairy business and some are still practising milkmen.

Mike and Naomi Hull didn't set out to collect milk bottles: he is a meteorologist at the London Weather Centre and she is head of English at King Alfred's School, north London.

It all began about eight years ago when the Express Dairy bought two small dairies in Dorset and started to use bottles from them for their own rounds. A Cricket Malherbie bottle was delivered to the Hulls' Highgate house by their milkman, Mr Herdman. They put it on a shelf above the cooker, asked around and found themselves involved in collecting. Now they have at least 13,000 bottles and it would be many more had they not weeded them out from time to time. 'Before this,' Mike Hull explained, 'milk bottles tended to be invisible, but once we started to look we

Above: Foreign milk bottles showing, from left to right, French, Brazilian, Belgian and Chinese examples.

found them to be far more interesting than we could have imagined. Our own milkman has been giving us unusual bottles for a long time.'

In an upper room, we were dazzled by a display of glittering glass. Bottles, under a variety of headings, were arranged on wide shelves. For the main part they are divided into counties. 'Old counties' – Naomi Hull was firm about this. 'We had a hell of a job finding a Rutland one.'

Slogans, pictures and advertisements on the bottles themselves make the array more colourful and less clinical than I had envisaged. One well-stocked shelf is labelled 'Mysteries'. Milk bottles travel a long way. 'That,' Mrs Hull admitted, 'is one of the excitements of it. If you take what used to be a main trunk road to Scotland you'll find bottles that have come from Cornwall or Devon – anywhere, for that matter. We go into woods and scrabble about. It's no good digging. They usually break. If we find one that's badly broken we note down the details and then chuck it away. Once in the Lake District we saw masses of Boy Scouts diligently clearing up every little bit of rubbish. Our hearts sank.' It was thrilling to meet a pair of real live litterbug champions.

I asked Mike Hull if he had ever been tempted to pinch a bottle from a doorstep. 'Yes, and I have yielded to the temptation,' he replied. 'An obsessive collector nearly always pinches something sooner or later.' Onlookers might be puzzled by the sight of this unlikely couple creeping up front steps rummaging for bottles.

Mike Hull, according to his wife, is the expert, and is steeped in milk-bottle history. 'The pattern changed in about 1860,' he told me, 'with the start of railways and the possibility of transporting milk. This tied in with outbreaks of foot-and-mouth and the necessity of carrying milk away from disease-free areas. Dairies tended to spring up round the main-line stations – Euston and Paddington. Most of these have been swallowed up now, although in places like Yorkshire there are still several dairies that are completely independent and bottling their own milk.'

Two milk-collector badges were pinned to the wall. The Hulls wear them for bottle shows so that people are aware of their quest. Now that there is more interest prices are going up, but they haven't stabilized and bargains can still be found. Fortunately for bottle enthusiasts the carton has turned out to be uneconomical. 'They first had a go at using cartons in the nineteen-thirties, but it didn't work. Cartons never come back, whereas on the whole milk bottles do.'

Although the British Isles are now considered to be TB-free, early publicity on the bottles tended to emphasize the safety of the milk. 'Three thousand kids a year used to die of TB. In 1932 a Brighton farmer used to sterilize his milk very carefully and then rinse out the bottles in sewage-contaminated water. The milk went to the dairy and was mixed with other milk, so that it reached a huge number of people.'

Mrs Hull indicated a 'horror' (a half-gallon container) that she found about five years ago in an American supermarket. Milk bottles have very nearly vanished in the United States, where there is a standard work for collectors (*Udder Delight* by John Tutton). On the whole milk bottles are valuable there, being more or less extinct. Garage sales prove good hunting-grounds.

With satisfaction the Hulls showed me a recent acquisition, a hundred-year-old American 'Thatcher'. It was very pretty: clear glass with a patent spring-loaded cap, and a design of a man wearing a hat and milking a benevolent cow. 'The moulding is lousy, which is why we could afford it.'

America first had the idea of giving bottles bulbous tops, a device to ensure (in theory, at any rate) that the cream came out first. One of the oddest American bottles is called 'the toothache' and boasts a particularly clever method of mixing the cream with the milk as it is poured. If you hold it in a certain way the neck appears to swell like a painful cheek.

Mike Hull has written an article on how to set about searching, recommending canal banks in particular. France can be fruitful. The Hulls showed me a bottle, found in a Paris flea-market, from a small village, now swallowed up by Paris. 'We couldn't find it on the map, so I had to get a French colleague to find the village for me.' It was in Paris, too, that they found a milk bottle from Germany – possibly a wartime bottle brought by a returning soldier.

They pondered over a Chinese bottle. 'This is curious: it's a current one and yet it has an old-fashioned top.'

Naomi Hull obtained a Russian bottle by way of a Swedish pen-friend. 'She's hooked. Every time

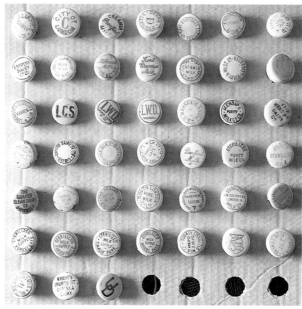

Pottery tops for sterilized bottles.

Left: Mr and Mrs Hull with their cat in the first-floor room which houses their milk bottle collection.

she goes to a new country she picks one up for me. She queued for this one for half an hour. Then she queued for another half-hour to pay, rushed back to the hotel and fished it out of her handbag. The beastly little top had come off and there was milk everywhere.'

Back in the British Isles section I was shown a milk bottle produced in 1929 by the National Milk Publicity Council with an inscription which ran: 'Fanny Fat and Susie Sugar for warmth and energy. Violet Vitamin for life and growth. Minnie Mineral for bones and teeth. Peter Protein for muscle.'

Then there was a sterilized English bottle of the 1920s with a ceramic spring-top; on it was a picture of a man in brightly patterned trousers. He'd taken off his top-hat and was saying, 'Madam, I am pure.' In an interesting later version he is no longer saying it; possibly there had been some legal quibble as to what was meant by the word 'pure'.

Naomi Hull (not a teacher of English for nothing) called out: 'Here, look at this: the apostrophe's in the wrong place.' She showed me a picture of a boy bowling a hoop and under this was written, 'For your childrens' sake'.

One dairyman, Clyde Higgs, made his bottles more interesting by having jingles printed on them. One reads: 'Oh Jubilee, Oh Jubilation, we drink a toast across the nation. For twenty-five years of grace and charm, purest milk from Clyde Higgs' farm.' His firm doesn't exist any more. 'That's the story of so many dairies. Look. Here's another one: "Milk and driving still surviving".'

I asked the Hulls how they reacted to bottle banks. 'They are deadly enemies. We have heard of dairymen who have just "banked" an entire collection.'

The Hulls' children used to be acutely embarrassed by their parents' innocent eccentricity, 'but now it's OK'.

As punctuation marks among the bottles are other milk-related objects: buckets, scoops, a Guernsey container, miniature milk-lorries and old cardboard bottle-tops. Cardboard tops went out in 1950 when aluminium ones came in. From a nail on the wall dangles a 1930s milk-order book. It was given to Mike and Naomi Hull by a dairy that had just been taken over, and it was full of milky messages: 'Pure rich milk', and 'Ruddy cheeks and sunny smiles. Nature's best gift – a healthy child'.

Every bottle is meticulously chronicled. Naomi Hull copies the designs into a catalogue and finds it 'very relaxing'. She longs for a milk float but they're not easy to come by, although she knows of two in a museum in Kent. If she ever acquires one she will use it for display in the middle of the bottle-lined room. It would be a worthy showcase for new additions to their already sensational collection.

Plastics

—SYLVIA KATZ—

Sylvia Katz is one of the foremost authorities on the history of plastics in Britain. She and her husband, architect and marathon runner Andrew Wright, have, in every corner of their north London house, a striking collection of plastic objects of every kind (from a 1930s cocktail shaker to shoe-horns and salad-servers moulded in celluloid) dating from the middle of the last century and recording the complex uses of plastic over the years.

The interest started when two 'rather at a loss' editors came to Sylvia Katz's degree show at Hornsey College of Art and commissioned her to write her first book, *Plastics, Designs and Materials* (1978). Her exposition of the chemistry of plastics in this book

Above: Sylvia Katz at a table in her conservatory, wearing a 100 per cent polystyrene jacket worked for the Queen's Silver Jubilee; she is surrounded by gleaming plastic objects.

was hailed by ICI as one of the clearest on the market. In her introduction she writes:

Many people, especially journalists and commentators, seem to think that we live in the 'Plastic Age'. In fact every decade since the modern plastics industry began in the 1920s has been hailed as the 'Plastic Age'. By rights that title is far more appropriate to those early years; new materials were being discovered at an increasing speed and the foundations of the industry as we know it were established.

In order to write this first book Sylvia Katz had to start from scratch; so she put on a white coat and attended a course on work machinery, maintaining that if she didn't understand plastics manufacture then nobody else would. When she qualified as a designer neither she nor her fellow students had been given any instruction on plastics. There was a huge gap there; owing to a shortage of teachers of the subject, the students simply had to pick things up as they went along.

As she gathered information for her first book she also began, with the help and encouragement of her husband, to collect pieces of plastic from every imaginable source: junk-shops, arcades, and the cupboards of friends and relations. In her view, one of the delights was to combine collecting with the writing of books. She also collects 'because it is vital to keep examples. We live in an age of throw-away items: tape-recorders, cassettes, hair-driers. Interesting designs are being replaced so quickly.'

Sylvia Katz's second book, *Classic Plastics: from Bakelite to High Tech*, is the first published guide to plastics collecting. It describes collections that can be visited and gives simple and safe home-tests for identification. It also suggests where help and advice can be found, gives names of dealers and restorers, provides guides to identification kits for schools, and has a very long and formidable list of trade-names and chemical constituents including such tongue-twisters as phenol formaldehyde, polymethyl methacrylate and polyvinyl chloride.

Although deeply involved in the subject herself, Miss Katz admits that 'plastic is a mysterious substance and many people are frightened of it. Nevertheless, the band of collectors is constantly expanding.'

She explains that, as in the case of so many other materials, plastics have had their setbacks. 'After the glorious swinging sixties, the seventies saw a bad patch for plastics. In 1973 came the dreadful oil crisis and the subsequent recession; plastics were particularly affected. All today's modern plastics are derived from oil, and between 1973 and 1979 oil prices quadrupled – affecting end-products and bringing to a close the age of cheap throw-away plastics.'

During the amazing eighties plastic has seen a comeback – much of it is now highly refined. Many examples, for instance the 'Incredible Edibles' (chocolates, biscuits, cakes), have great practical uses. One is in the training of cabin staff on aircraft, who learn their skills while using trays of plastic food; another is in window-dressing, particularly in confectioners' shops where the chocolates won't melt in the sunlight.

Laminates, too, have returned and designers are busy developing very exciting ideas, many coming from Italy.

'Plastic' is still sometimes used as a word of abuse by journalists, but Miss Katz thinks that the rude term 'plastic people' dates back to the early days of films and the world of celluloid.

Sylvia Katz spread a large strip of bright green plastic lawn, Astroturf, over her conservatory table. She uses this for 'indoor picnics' in wet weather and, flanked by two palms in pots, it is not impossible to imagine yourself to be outside. All round the house are plastic dolls, coffee-pots, wireless sets, old telephones and disposable oxygen masks. Sylvia Katz held up for my inspection a carrier-bag advertising Colorcore – a new type of material, launched in America in 1983, that has spawned a lot of designs. An innovation rather like solid Formica, it can be worked or carved like timber and is an important name for the future.

Wearing a jacket made from 100 per cent polystyrene (worked for the Queen's Silver Jubilee), Sylvia Katz drew attention to 'a piece of plastic knitting sculpture', representing a *cache-sexe* of unfinished knitting held together by two large needles.

Living among gleaming plastic objects, products of the machine age, Sylvia Katz delights in the realization that 'most plastics, being the ultimate outcome of oil and coal – rotting trees and vegetation – go back to prehistoric days; to the beginning of life on earth'.

In front are two Belplastic pots with various beakers of mottled phenolic, 1920s.
Behind these are a variety of objects, including a coffee grinder, a Bandalasta powder bowl,
a silver-rimmed urn and nesting horns in alabaster mottled Beatl urea thiourea formaldehyde.

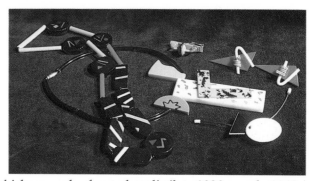

Left: In front are napkin rings in the form of ducks and chickens made of cast phenolic (late 1930s–early 1940s)
and behind these are a number of other plastic items such as, a yellow sugar shaker,
two Quickmix egg-flip mixers and a yellow and black cruet set.

Right: Clockwise from the left are, two necklaces designed by Pat Thornton for Cicada in
acrylic rod and cast polyester pieces, inlaid with polyester resin; tie-pin made of tubing and coloured acrylic,
designed by John Hughes, 1979; pair of ear-rings of acrylic and painted metal rod, 1979;
brooch of laminated Formica and nylon string, designed by Louise Slater, 1985.

Lady Lambton in her Chelsea bedroom
which has a butterfly-patterned carpet especially designed for the owner.

Butterflies

— VISCOUNTESS LAMBTON —

Pendant necklace, brooches and rings spread multi-coloured wings over Lady Lambton's butterfly-patterned shirt, adding sparkle to her statuesque beauty.

Her house, one of the oldest in the King's Road, Chelsea, appears at first sight to be tall and narrow, promising many floors, but when you work your way around a corner and emerge from under the stairs you find yourself in an unexpectedly high room with three tall windows leading out, beyond butterfly-fashioned straw door-mats, to a mirror-reflected garden. The high, light room could be mistaken for a gigantic butterfly-house.

Pointing to a metal container, Lady Lambton stopped for a moment. 'I'm wondering whether to cover this face-case with "butts". It came by post. I'll have to, won't I? It's awful as it is.'

Lady Lambton has always collected butterflies. They are everywhere. Picture-frames, vases and chair-covers are all butterfly printed, painted or stamped. 'This is a useful thing. Look. An inflated rubber butterfly bracelet. I was going to wear it for a memorial service, but the children said, "Certainly not. Don't be facetious."'

The sofa is stacked with cushions, hand-painted in lepidopterous designs. These were given to Lady Lambton by Lord Wilton, who said, 'I want you to know that these were not printed by the yard. They were painted especially for you.'

On a table stands a mandolin inlaid with mother-of-pearl butterflies. Lady Lambton picked it up: 'I want to polish it but it would be useless to use one of those spray polishes. Fatal.' She unfolded a butterfly-spattered umbrella and explained, 'I had an absolute haul in Japan.'

I asked her if she was knowledgeable about butterflies in general. 'I know them by sight,' she replied, 'but I'm not too keen on the chloroform bottle.'

On the mantelpiece stand two Charles Addams cartoons, drawn for her. 'I had a terrible motor

Above: Two butterfly cartoons drawn for Lady Lambton by Charles Addams.

accident and went to hospital for two and a half years. Look. There's the surgeon. First he opens me up and then, in the second one, out flies an enormous butterfly.'

Butterfly prints cover walls on the stairway, leading down to the kitchen where even the oven-gloves are butterfly-shaped. They vie for space with washing-up cloths, Tiffany plates and jam-jars, all enlivened by antennae and wings. Notes pinned to the fridge are secured by magnetic butterflies beside paper ones placed there for ornament. Several are stuck to the window-panes. There are saucepans, teapots and egg-cups, all decorated with butterflies, and a piece of raffia-work containing clothes-pegs, butterfly-topped. 'I hate that,' the owner confessed. On the ironing-board was spread a butterfly-patterned table-cloth. 'My daughter Beatrix says that sometimes I sacrifice quality for quantity.' Here she drew my attention to a sundae-dish that nestled among a collection of tea-caddies.

On a half-landing leading to the first floor, we stopped by a brocade-covered table. 'That's Queen Anne. Some of it wore out so I stitched "butts" on the faded bits.' I peered closely and my hostess said, 'Thank God you can't see them. It means that they can't be too obvious.'

On the floor of the bedroom lies a butterfly-patterned carpet, designed for the room. Against the wall was propped a butterfly-shaped fly-swatter. 'They've started already, you know.' Had there been a fly it would have been eclipsed by winged calendars, bags, buckles and appliqué pillowcases. Heaped on the dressing-table was a jumble of hair-clips, rings and hat-pins, all with butterfly connections. Propped up behind these was a butterfly picture painted by Lady Lambton's daughter Anne, and a framed embroidered one given to her by Lucien Freud – 'I don't know why.'

Lady Lambton revealed that John Julius Norwich has a unicorn tattooed upon his person. 'They're his mother's, Diana Cooper's, favourites. I do call that an act of love. I don't see my son Ned having a "butt" tattooed on him anywhere.'

Lady Lambton wound up a spring hidden beneath a pair of artificial wings, held it high and let it go. It whirled through the room, out through the door and disappeared round a bend in the stairway. 'It baffles the pigeons when I let it loose from the balcony.'

In the bathroom, where, again, the curtains were specially designed, Lady Lambton's dressing-gown (butterfly-patterned) lay spread over a chair near the bath – which was garnished with butterfly face-flannels and make-up jars.

'There's no point in showing you my wardrobe. It's all butterflies. My daughter Beatrix knitted me this jumper.' Rows and rows of 'butts'. 'I hope there aren't any moths. They give me the jim-jams.' She has a mass of butterfly hats; one straw one is entirely decorated with tin wings. Shoes? 'Yes. Shoes galore. Mostly for summer; those ones with butterflies which hold sandals together.'

In the drawing-room Maria, a spirited Portuguese lady who helps in the house, poured coffee into butterfly-handled cups as we sat beside the fire and cast her eyes to heaven. 'One day when I finish working here two butterflies will carry me home. I'm butterfly-sick.'

On the back of one of the many brooches on Lady Lambton's shirt are engraved the words, 'Presented to Mrs Drummond-Hay by members of the war-work depot in Brazil'.

'But you're not Mrs Drummond-Hay,' I pointed out, 'so how did you come by it?'

'No. I wasn't in the World War One work depot in Brazil either. Chiquita Astor gave it to me. She found it somewhere.'

Lady Lambton revealed that she has 'stacks and stacks of butterfly spectacles stuffed away in drawers', but the children won't let her wear them. 'They say that they make me look like Dame Edna Everage.'

Sir Arthur Conan Doyle

—*RICHARD LANCELYN GREEN*—

Richard Lancelyn Green started to take an interest in Sherlock Holmes when he was a boy and attended his first meeting of the Sherlock Holmes Society when he was eleven, becoming a member by the age of twelve.

He soon began collecting editions of Holmes stories and, not many years later, embarked on compiling a bibliography of the works of Conan Doyle which was given an Edgar Allan Poe award. While engaged on this task, Green says, 'I found more and

Above: Richard Lancelyn Green in Sherlock Holmes's sitting room at 221B Baker Street.

more evidence of the extraordinary power and the curious reality which emanate from the great detective. Sherlock Holmes is very "real" in a way which is not common, and one tends to fall into what Eliot called "the fancy of his existence".'

Unlike most Sherlockians, Green does not restrict his studies to the Holmes stories because he feels that to appreciate them fully one should know as much as possible about Conan Doyle himself. Ultimately, he says, truth is more interesting than fiction, even if it is not always as entertaining, and Conan Doyle was a remarkable person.

Besides his intense interest and his erudite literary output, Green has built up a scholarly library and collection of artwork, manuscripts, letters and photographs relating to Conan Doyle – most of which are kept at Poulton Hall, the Cheshire house which incorporates a variety of architectural styles, and in which Green's family have lived since the eleventh century.

In addition to related postcards, film-stills, scripts, posters, menu-cards, Sherlockian journals, cigarette-cards (including ones issued in 1936 by the Spanish Spiritualist Federation), there are early fliers – among them original advertisement slips for *A Study in Scarlet*, *The Hound of the Baskervilles* and *The Return of Sherlock Holmes*.

Green's collection is unquestionably comprehensive but, when he is asked if anything is lacking, he replies, 'My goodness me, yes. Collecting becomes a habit which is ever more demanding and which can never be satisfied. There are certain books that I would dearly like to have: an original of *Beeton's Christmas Annual* for 1887 with the first Sherlock Holmes story, or the first separate edition of that book which was issued the following year. These are very hard to find. Above all, I am looking for a perfect copy of each book. Ideally this would be in its original dust-jacket and inscribed by the author to someone of importance. Original artwork would also be very welcome: drawings by Sidney Paget, for example. And it would be highly gratifying to own the manuscript of a story – preferably one about Sherlock Holmes.'

While compiling the bibliography, Green acquired the wide knowledge of his subject that enables him to recognize rare books when he sees them. His greatest satisfaction, however, comes from adding to his own knowledge and learning from others. His interest in the subject has also led him to deeply valued friendships both with Conan Doyle's daughter, Lady Bromet, and with his nephew, Brigadier John Doyle.

One of the attics at Poulton Hall has been turned into a reconstruction of Sherlock Holmes's sitting-room at 221B Baker Street. Green embarked on this remarkable project when he was twelve, translating, piece by piece, the fruits of Conan Doyle's vivid descriptive powers.

In this small top room, cluttered but not shabby, any knowledgeable Sherlockian would immediately recognize a number of familiar objects: the gasogene (an early form of soda-syphon) on the sideboard; the cigars in the coal-scuttle; the Persian slipper containing Holmes's tobacco; the unanswered correspondence fixed to the centre of the mantelpiece by a jack-knife. To the right of the door is Watson's picture of General Gordon and, leaning on his books on the other side, the unframed picture of Henry Ward Beecher. Many other objects meet the eye – a cluster of bones used in a case that Holmes was working on, the table in the corner displaying Holmes's scientific experiments and the low-powered microscope over which he once leant. Then there is his basket chair and the bearskin hearth-rug, on to which Doctor Thorneycroft Huxtable collapsed in so dramatic a fashion at the start of the Priory School case. Against Holmes's chair lies his Stradivarius violin 'which he bought very cheaply'.

It is worth looking even more closely. The mantelpiece and the ornate overmantel with its two fine gas-brackets is a good place to start. Here is a photograph of Irene Adler (who to Holmes would always be *the* woman), the torn message which played such an important part in *The Reigate Puzzle* and the invitation to the Gas-Fitters' Ball (made out to Mr and Mrs Windibank). There is a dark lantern, Watson's hip-flask, a cast of the engineer's thumb and an opium

*Opposite: The sitting room at 221B Baker Street showing, amongst other Holmes-related items,
his low-powered microscope, Watson's despatch boxes and the Persian slipper in which Holmes kept his tobacco.*

pipe used by Holmes (although he did not actually smoke opium).

Continuing the tour, one sees Holmes's hypodermic needle and his seven per cent solution of cocaine. There are medals awarded to him, dottles of tobacco, a telegram, a police whistle and other such oddments. Lying in the hearth is the bent poker (bent by Dr Grimesby Roylott and straightened by Holmes). On a pile of Holmes's books is coiled the speckled band itself and, near this, a cane table loaded with scrapbooks on which sits one of Watson's tin despatch boxes neatly inscribed 'John H. Watson MD, late of the Indian Army'. On the box stands a stuffed bird – for a long time thought to be the trained cormorant. Passing to the desk there is a wealth of unusual material: the notice announcing the dissolution of the Red-Headed League and a small brass salver with visiting-cards on it (one belonging to Charles Augustus Milverton, another to Lady Frances Carfax and one of Holmes's own special cards bearing the name of Dr Hill Barton). There are also a pair of pince-nez, a message bearing the initials 'KKK', a scrap of paper marked with small dancing men and some blotting paper showing a barely distinguishable message in reverse. There is a label from the goose that carried the blue carbuncle and two fine photographs of the horse Silver Blaze.

On the table in front of Holmes's chair there are copies of his own pamphlets, and there is even a magazine containing his early articles on deduction which Watson tapped in disbelief with his egg-spoon, leaving yellow stains on it.

Everywhere there is evidence of Holmes's interest in detection, even small pill-boxes housing tobacco ash and other samples.

There is a phonograph (which Watson described as a gramophone in *The Mazarin Stone*) and a fine magic lantern with attendant boxes of glass slides.

On a carved wooden easel is propped a painting by Lord Leighton. Sherlock Holmes picked that up on a visit to the Royal Academy. By the door there is a stand containing the alpenstock which Holmes left at the Reichenbach Falls, and other canes and riding crops including a sword-stick used by Colonel Sebastian Moran.

There is much more besides in this tiny attic room. It contains Holmes's fencing foil and his boxing-gloves; Watson's revolver, his brother's watch with the pawnbroker's marks in evidence, his Gladstone bag and his top-hat with the stethoscope inside. There is a battered billycock, a dumb-bell, a sponge covered in make-up and a lock of auburn hair – all of which, no doubt, would be familiar to those who have followed Sherlock Holmes's career.

To enter this world of meticulous re-enactment is to wonder if one has arrived in the middle of a game of Chinese Whispers. After all, even if readers are forced to agree that Sherlock Holmes did not exactly exist, his room (after a fashion) did.

Conan Doyle, in his lodgings at Southsea in the 1880s, had a table of chemicals laid out for his medical work and possibly for his photographic experiments. Certainly he had scrapbooks and commonplace books and paraphernalia that he later used when describing Holmes's room in Baker Street.

Sir Arthur Conan Doyle, by firm believers often accused of the heartless murder of Sherlock Holmes, would be gratified to visit (perhaps with the assistance of spiritualists, in whose powers he strongly believed) Green's conscientiously reconstructed setting for the hero born out of Conan Doyle's own imagination. This is not to say that his creator did not arrive at a point when he was anxious to extinguish his detective. On 9 August 1893 he is reported to have said, 'I am tired of Sherlock Holmes and am going to find a suitable place in which to kill him.'

Opposite: Another corner of Sherlock Holmes's sitting room showing other Holmes-related objects.

The Mander & Mitchenson
Theatre Collection

Joe Mitchenson has lived in his house in south-east London for over sixty years. He and his mother, who adored the theatre, moved there when he was thirteen and he remembers being sick with excitement at the time. Over the years he has seen vast changes in the neighbourhood; houses come down and go up – but Mitchenson still recalls the good old days when women scrubbed the front steps on a Saturday.

Mitchenson comes from a theatrical family. His father was a dramatic critic, his grandfather an actor, and the rest of the family went into the theatre in some guise or other. As he grew up his instincts were for theatre things. There were reminders all around the house: books, photographs, programmes and posters. These always fascinated him and, as well as obsessively building model theatres from glue and

Opposite: Looking through to the sitting-room with busts of Charles Wyndham and George Robey.
A series of Agatha Walker theatrical figures stand on the bookcase.

Above: Joe Mitchenson among his treasures – including a china figure of David Garrick as Richard III.

paper, he was bursting to go on the stage from a very early age.

He began training as a dancer when he was a small boy, but in those days it didn't do for a dancer to be as long-limbed as he became so he went on to Fay Compton's drama school in the early thirties. After this he was given a walk-on part in the West End and struck up a friendship with Alec Guinness, who was making his first appearance (also as a walk-on) in the same play.

At this point Mitchenson started to collect in a 'not very serious way'. He didn't do it deliberately until 1939 when he met the late Raymond Mander, who had had a similar career and had also started collecting. 'Things were very black in 1939. It was a horrible time,' he remembers.

The pair, later known in theatre circles as 'the Boys', met in a production and discovered their common interest. Mitchenson was called up for a few years, was invalided out of the army and eventually re-met Mander, whereupon they decided to join forces and pool their theatrical 'things'. At the start they thought that they would like to have a theatre museum which would also be a theatre; to run it as a club and to put on forgotten plays of the last century. This didn't work out and the collection became a collection pure and simple. Their next idea was to write a book on the subject. They started with *Hamlet through the Ages* and they went on to write more than twenty books as they built up their collection.

This consists of absolutely everything to do with the theatre. All objects in the house, excepting some pieces of furniture, have a theatrical connection. Noel Coward in his will left a dressing-gown apiece to Mander and Mitchenson and, on display in a cabinet, is a souvenir of Coward's seventieth birthday party held at the Savoy Hotel. This is a life-sized cuffed hand holding a cigarette in spun sugar. There was one at the centre of every table at the party, but

View of the sitting room showing a bust of Sir Charles Wyndham in the window. Among other items is a painting of David Garrick in 'The Wonder', and, above it, a painting of Julian L'Estrange acting in a one-line part in 'As You Like It'. There are many china figures of famous actors and actresses, both in the alcove and on the mantelpiece.

*Pollocks model theatre of the 1850s showing a harlequinade. On the shelves,
with the theatrical books, are Gilbert and Sullivan china figures of the 1940s.*

eight guests surrounded each table so there was something of a fight about who was going to bear away each hand. The people at Mitchenson's table were very generous and said that he must have it but, as he carried it triumphantly off, Frankie Howerd bumped into him and knocked the cigarette askew – providing yet another theatrical reminder.

Each room in the house, stuffed to bursting point like a Victorian parlour, is lined and loaded with busts, portraits and commemorative ware. Tinsel

figures of the 1840s, made by children and very glittery, Berlin woolwork and stage designs crowd every cranny. Great actors and actresses appear in their most elegant roles: Terry, Irving, Kemble and Beerbohm Tree. All top theatrical people, as well as many minor ones, have given or left something to the collection. On a shelf sits a handbag used by Vivien Leigh in *A Streetcar Named Desire*.

Figures fashioned to honour star performances (a custom that died out after the last war) abound in the

The theatre magazine room containing periodicals and magazines, including 'Opera', 'Theatre World', 'Plays and Players' and 'Ballet'.

house. Joe Mitchenson is particularly attached to Agatha Walker's model of Peter Pan as played by Jean Forbes Robertson. When first he saw the play Mitchenson was bowled over by it but said to his mother, 'I loved that play but I can't see why a lady has to have the part. I hope that when I get a bit older I'll get it.' There are several such models of Dame Edith Evans. Mitchenson loves the figure of her in *The Merry Wives of Windsor*. 'It's so like her,' he says. 'She was a good friend although reputed to be very

mean. I never thought that. It was simply that she started so humbly that money meant a great deal to her.' He remembers one day in particular when she came to lunch carrying a very large and tarty handbag. He longed for her to produce the imperishable phrase, 'A *handbag*!' but she never did. Later she confessed to loathing the part of Lady Bracknell in *The Importance of Being Earnest*. Mitchenson challenged her with the compliment, 'Think of the wretched actress who had to play it after you!'

Walls in the Mitchenson house are heavy with portraits of immortals like Mrs Siddons and David Garrick. China figures by the score (including one of an animal trainer who so intrigued Queen Victoria that she went regularly to see him at Drury Lane, ignoring Macready who was playing at the same theatre and who suffered deep mortification as a result) mix with an original set design for *The Mousetrap* and the Spangled Order of the Elephant worn by John Philip Kemble as Hamlet. Even lavatory doors are decorated with name-plates from stars' dressing-rooms.

The heart of the collection comprises letters, diaries, prompt-books and gramophone records, which form the basis of a research information service. These archives are available to any genuine enquirer and the collection has supplied material for over eight hundred books, numerous stage productions, radio and television programmes and films.

More than a decade ago the collection, already overflowing its South Bank base, was scheduled to be incorporated in the National Theatre complex. Alas, the theatre's director, Sir Peter Hall, said that the space was needed for car parks and offices. The blow was a bitter one, but more bitter still was the local council's simultaneous decree that the Mander and Mitchenson home was to be demolished. 'The Boys' rejected offers to re-house their collection, took the matter to court – and won. From then on the tide turned. In 1977 the collection became a registered charity with Lord Olivier as President.

Recently Lewisham Council has given the charity a Georgian mansion at a peppercorn rent and gradually the objects are to be moved there. It will be open to the public at convenient hours and the contents will be available to students – a service that will be easier to arrange than in a private house.

Joe Mitchenson hopes to spend a lot of time there.

He doesn't want to fade out of the picture but to go on till he drops. He will always be around doing something or other. As he grows older he plans to work a little less and to have a little more assistance. Already he has a very helpful voluntary staff – ladies who come in to keep costumes in good repair and so on. It is indeed sad that Raymond Mander is no longer alive to see the collection become a museum – not that it will be known as such. Mitchenson hates the word 'museum' (as did Mander), having always found it 'a bit stuffy'.

The collection's transfer, under the aegis of a young and professional curator, Colin Mabberley, represents the fulfilment of a wish made by both Mander and Mitchenson, that their much-cherished treasures should belong to the nation. Joe Mitchenson looks forward to seeing the mansion as a cultural centre filled not merely with theatrical memorabilia but also with the sounds of poetry and music. He would like an elegant restaurant to be opened there, and hopes one day to see the neglected lake refilled.

Perhaps some of the magic of intimacy will be lost when the collection is moved to Beckenham Place but, since the plan is to decorate it as a country house owned by theatre enthusiasts rather than as a set of displays and since Joe Mitchenson will be prompting from the wings, it is probable that a new but equally evocative atmosphere will be created.

Lord Olivier, writing on the subject of the opening of Beckenham Place, says: 'Mander and Mitchenson's work as collectors, scholars, historians and archivists for the theatrical profession and for the whole entertainment industry is unique. Its impact and importance is world-wide. The collection which they have amassed is as extraordinary as their generosity in donating it to the charity which I now ask you to support.'

British Police Equipment

—MERVYN MITTON—

Mervyn Mitton, ex-policeman, collector, author and herbalist, hangs his Police Retirement Notice on the wall of his Dorset sitting-room. It reads 'Conduct Exemplary'. 'I wouldn't have put it up there if it had said otherwise,' he points out.

Mitton joined the Police Force because he had a deep and longstanding interest in it and is convinced that 'most people join because they are dedicated. At least they used to be. Nowadays it's so well paid that it's considered to be a good bread-winning job.'

Although Mitton much enjoyed his work on the beat in London's East End (where he had a very high arrest rate and won five commendations), he left the force when his father died and his mother needed his help in running a thriving family business as herbalists – Cathay of Bournemouth.

Mitton says that until recently the history of the police has been much neglected. 'Every day, nine out of ten newspaper reports involve the police in some way. They enter everyone's lives and yet little is known of the origin of the force.' He has put this right with the publication of his own book, *The Policeman's Lot*. It is a carefully researched volume and Mitton is confident that it is the definitive work on the subject,

Above: Mr Mitton holding a standard-pattern constabulary police hanger, c. 1850.
This one was issued to the Barrow-in-Furness Borough Police.

although he admits ruefully that it will help to make truncheons and tipstaves highly desirable as collector's pieces and will probably push their price up.

Although Mitton keeps a few of his police trophies in the office above his shop, the bulk of his collection of British police equipment lives in his streamlined house (surrounded by fountains, sundials, aviaries and immaculately tended lawns) nearby. Drawers, cupboards and cabinets are weighed down with truncheons, tipstaves, helmets, whistles and keys.

Anyone who assumes that a truncheon is simply a stocky, round-ended stick used by Constable Plod to conk an unsuspecting felon over the head would have to revise his ideas if fortunate enough to visit this rarefied collection.

There is nothing that Mervyn Mitton does not know about the truncheon. Until 1829 there was no

Above: Various items including Bullseye police lanterns, a pistol used by Birmingham police in the 1860s, an early watchman's rattle and various tipstaves and truncheons.

Right: A selection of tipstaves and truncheons dating from between 1750 and 1870.

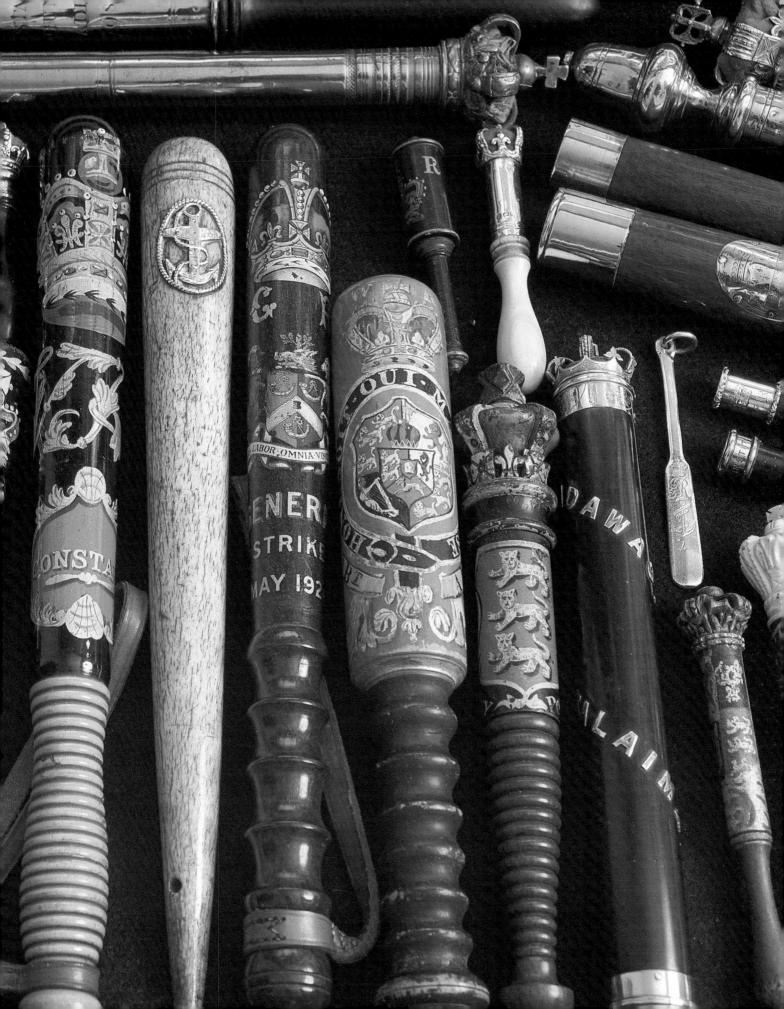

such thing as a police uniform and the truncheon was a badge of office. Each constable would have to pay for his own, and would usually commission his local furniture-maker to make it. For this reason many truncheons look like turned wooden chair-legs. From the carpenter's shop the officer would go in search of a craftsman-artist who could decorate his truncheon. Some of these examples of painted truncheons are very skilled and others are primitive, depending on talent in the area. Mitton has many hundreds of truncheons both on display and stored away in his meticulously tidy house which, he insists, is his home and not a museum. He restricts his collection to specific parts of appropriate rooms, thus preventing it from taking over.

Until the 1920s truncheons were usually highly decorated and many bore the owner's initials as well as crowns, coats-of-arms and clues to the function of the particular officer. The truncheon of the Special Constable for the Corn Exchange, for example, is painted with a reaper and scythe. Specialized Victorian riot truncheons have screw tops so that they could be attached to poles and thus keep rioters at a distance. A knob could be pressed to release a sharp and lethal blade in the event of extreme violence. Mitton's own truncheon, issued to him when he joined the force, is over a hundred years old and made of heavy lignum vitae, a South American hardwood. 'It still bears the marks of a car window that I had to smash,' says Mitton.

Tipstaves – staffs or sticks usually tipped with metal – denote various degrees of authority: they have been used by a high official of the London Docks, or an inspector of pavements and sewers, or a bailiff. Mitton keeps his best tipstaff specimens, with intricate carvings and crown-shaped tips, in a glass-topped cabinet in his bedroom 'because I like to look at them and because it's a unique collection – more than a collection. These tipstaves were actually used for peacekeeping in this country.'

During his time as a constable on the beat, Mitton staged an exhibition in Bethnal Green entitled 'The London Police and the East End'. Trunks full of police equipment were unearthed and sent along. Many of the owners of these items had no further use for them and that is how Mitton came to start his own collection. Characteristically detective-like,

he became an expert on dating and deciphering. 'Although possession is, of course, part of the fun, the real thrill is in research and in using one's knowledge to trace an object back, in some cases, to a particular officer.'

Mitton has deliberately refrained from hoarding many uniforms because 'they take up too much space and gather moths and dust', but there is a formidable line-up of hats and helmets. He explains that 'the very first policemen wore top-hats – the idea being that they didn't want to look like a paramilitary force. Later, when this policy changed, they began to copy the military style of the period. A flat shape was adopted for police hats when cars came in. A police officer will sometimes wear his flat hat for driving a Panda and will still keep his helmet on the seat beside him.'

Swords provide another glittering section of the Mitton collection. These were given to constables if they were working in dangerous areas, or in graveyards when body-snatching was rife. There were many occasions in Victorian times when police drew their swords and charged as a body.

Hats and helmets, backed by reward notices from outside old police stations, perch on top of cabinets that shelter fingerprint sets of the 1870s, complete with black and grey powder. Above these are a pair of prison keys and a giant ball and chain weighing 50 lb, once the property of an old man who didn't know what to do with them and who sent them along to Mervyn Mitton's suitable repository. Both came from Bellevue Prison, Manchester, which was pulled down in 1894.

Mervyn Mitton is determined not to leave his collection to a museum, where it would only be stuffed away in some dark corner. He thinks that it would be more fun if it were to be sold and circulated, giving other collectors the chance to own some of his rare and esoteric pieces.

Mitton's house, up a tarmac drive and hidden from the road, is decorated with tubs of fuchsias and swinging baskets hanging from the porch. It is well protected by burglar alarms, closed-circuit television, and a switch by the owner's bed that activates floodlighting in house and grounds in case of disturbance; it is not unlike a Hollywood version of a police station.

Toy Soldiers

—JAMES OPIE—

In his introductory passage to the Toy Soldier Exhibition of 1984–5 at the London Toy and Model Museum, James Opie wrote:

Toy soldiers represent in miniature one of the darkest sides of humanity, our propensity to organize specialist groups of killers to impose our collective will upon others. Yet it is every man's right to fight for as much as he has, and to defend what is his. This seems to be an ingrained instinct. Modern society provides peace for most of us through asking some of us to become soldiers, and this is probably the most beneficial solution that can be devised at present within the known disadvantages forced on our existence by human nature.

Toys are both amusing and instructive, and most children's play helps to increase their understanding of the adult world with which they must one day come to terms. Toy soldiers, therefore, represent the qualities of courage, loyalty, devotion and self-sacrifice that are associated with the soldier in real life, and even help to prepare the way to a comprehension of the reasons for wounding and death in war. So fundamental is the place of the soldier in any civilization to date that in spite of any well-meaning idealism to the contrary, toy soldiers refuse to disappear, even under the current avalanche of electronic playthings, and merely reassert their importance in different guises, for instance as 'Action Man' in the 1970s and the enormously popular 'Star Wars' figures of the 1980s.

James Opie, owner of about 30,000 toy soldiers, is the son of Peter and Iona Opie and elder brother of Robert. He claims to be partly responsible for having been 'born into a collection'. Before his birth his parents decided to collect together some nursery rhymes in time for his arrival. However, they were unable to find any definitive work on the subject, and took the idea of producing one themselves to Oxford University Press. They were encouraged to pursue the project and as a result they jointly compiled *The Oxford Book of Nursery Rhymes*. That took off and was followed by a collection of children's folk-lore.

James Opie's interest in toy soldiers began at the age of four when he was first given a group made from home-cast solid lead. His grandmother's carpenter had moulded them and they were treated to two coats of paint, one by his grandmother and one by himself.

Above: Pre-First World War toy soldiers made by Britains Ltd. A group of rare Territorial Infantry in red and blue uniforms and peaked hats with mounted officer, dated 24 February 1910. They were probably made for the coronation of King George V when troops in these uniforms took part in the celebrations.

Since then the passion has passed through an enormous number of phases. When Opie was a boy it was usual to make a collection based on a particular theme. From the age of about eight or nine he played war-games with a friend, with whom he came to an agreement: whatever sort of toy soldier was purchased by one couldn't be purchased by the other. They eventually found themselves in an arms race – they would independently rush out to the shops and buy every kind of soldier they could possibly find. Opie then became interested in a diversity of related subjects. Toy soldiers led on to arms and armament. Later he began to look into the causes of war, making a study of those countries that invented and amassed armaments.

At university James Opie read military history and the origins of war; although this was to provide a background to his life, he was equally interested in toys – following more closely his parents' interests than the subject of war itself.

His parents encouraged him to 'do his own thing' and didn't offer specific help, his father only insisting that whenever he collected anything, he should write down what it was, where he found it and how much it cost. Opie admits that it's very tempting not to bother, but on the rare occasions when he has yielded to temptation he has always regretted it. His father also taught Opie that knowledge of his subject is more important, in one way, than the models he collects. Opie now sees himself as someone who knows about toy soldiers rather than as someone who owns a lot of them. He maintains that it is vital to ensure that the collection doesn't become more significant than the collector. If you feel that you could no longer get rid of it happily, then you're caught by it and it's taking over your life. He is convinced that, if he had to, he could dispose of his collection tomorrow because records of it exist and because if he ever came into enough money to reassemble it he could do so. It has been a part of his life; he's done it, and if anything disastrous happens it would not be the end of the world.

Armies invade every cranny of the Opies' Egham house. An attic room is entirely given over to a toy world. Here, buildings are all either commercially made or constructed from kits, some from an Italian castle-building system and some from 'Architects' (described by the London Museum as 'the only example of a toy trying to reproduce the building methods of the 1950s'). All these are roughly in scale with the soldiers and are put together to create a convincing townscape. Marks and Spencer, hospitals and churches provide a background for the regiments. The two principal ones on show happen to be Opie's favourites: the Royal Welch Fusiliers in a column marching across the 'town', and the Royal Scots Greys who clatter up the back streets. Opie's collection lives up to his theory that the bigger the collection, the more scope you have. 'That's the beauty of it. If you're going to make a display you're not going to want just one soldier marching along. You want a whole platoon or battalion. There's not much fun in collecting toy soldiers unless you're going to show them off in a dramatic way. That is where the spectacular part of it comes in. There's an urge not just to collect one team of Royal Horse Artillery but a battery or two batteries.'

Where, then, does Opie limit himself? 'Any collection can get too large when it's filled the available space or consumed the available cash. I simply say OK: my favourite bits are this, that and t'other, so let's get rid of the rest and use the proceeds to build up any sections that are lacking.'

Opie has made it a rule that toy soldiers should not be his business in a primary sense, that he should not depend on them for his bread and butter. If he had to do that he might be forced to get rid of something he really wanted to keep; and if he was always working on them he might get surfeited with them and that would make life unbearable. At the moment he is busy reorganizing, rationalizing and listing what he has.

A back room on the first floor is used as an office. Prints and reproductions hang on the walls above rows of red boxes all neatly labelled: 'Spanish Police', 'German Infantry', and so on. It is in this room that Opie's books are written. He has a publishing programme of four books, each of which has a particular purpose. His first is a handbook on his hobby – what it is and why people enjoy it. The second is a price guide to objects you might find in junk-shops, and is designed to give readers a taste of the various things they might collect if they had a mind to. The third may be his *chef-d'œuvre* – he thought no one would be brave enough to publish it; it is a detailed compendium of the first forty years of Britains Ltd. Britains

James Opie examining the underside of a figure with an illuminated magnifying glass. He is standing in front of a wall full of storage boxes, some of which are open on the sorting and display table in front of him. On the left can be seen Skybird airfield buildings and on the right a regiment of Britains small-size gun teams.

are still the major British manufacturers of toy soldiers. Because many firms pirated their designs, from 1900 to 1913 they signed and dated the base of each toy in order to be able to invoke copyright laws. Opie has a box of theirs, dated 1 February 1901, on which is printed the firm stricture: 'Don't buy worthless copies of our English models. None genuine without our above signature on box.' It is signed 'W. Britain' in facsimile handwriting.

Opie's latest acquisition – a set of genuine Britain soldiers – was designed, he thinks, for the Coronation of King George V and is thought to be the newly-formed territorial regiments. They appeared at that Coronation for the first time in specially designed uniforms – blue peaked caps and red-and-blue coats. They are rare and, as far as Opie knows, no such group has turned up at auction before.

James Opie's passion for Lego is a separate story. Being a science-fiction fan he is fascinated by space construction and is building a fleet of Lego space-empire-type vehicles. The one in front of him is a multicoloured marine landing vehicle, rather like an aircraft carrier, with retractable turrets and various detachable spaceships that amalgamate to form the whole. His son Philip also collects Lego, and recently the whole family visited Lego-Land in Denmark. Opie's daughter Elizabeth collects heart-shaped boxes. The only comment that Avryll, James Opie's wife, has made about collecting is: 'It keeps them at home and it isn't drink!'

The Pack Age Revisited

— ROBERT OPIE —

Surprising the world by entering it in a taxi-cab en route for the nursing-home, Robert Opie is continuing to astonish it. Historian and sociologist as well as collector, Opie has built, and is still building, a living collection spanning over a century – a tribute to changing industry.

His collection comprises some 250,000 items – tins, bottles, packets, advertisements and posters – all meticulously indexed and mostly fitted into his house in West London where, not surprisingly, he lives alone.

Recently Opie has moved about five per cent of this collection to a newly-opened museum, nostalgically christened 'The Pack Age Revisited'. This is to be found in the Albert Warehouse in the inland port at Gloucester.

In the entrance hall, within earshot of a video blaring out a thirty-year span of screened advertisements, is a framed notice, signed by Opie, for the information of visitors:

This exhibition is a tribute to those who for over a hundred years have given their talent and ingenuity, their dedication and service and their creative and artistic abilities to the Age of the Pack. Such is their achievement that today we have available an incredible choice of products that are carefully packed, steadily distributed, actively promoted and competitively priced.

In the exhibition are goods which, since Victorian times, have crowded the shelves of Britain's grocers, sweet-shops, chemists, tobacconists, pubs and the earliest supermarkets. From these objects you can trace the changes in social tempo, the whims of style and fashion, the advent of the family car, the jazz age, the gradual emancipation of women, the disappearance of the domestic servant and the radical changes in shopping habits – all of which are reflected in the everyday products people have bought over the years.

Robert Opie among large biscuit tins
with decorative paper labels.

A selection of custard tins.

Some of the household polishes which have helped the weekly chore during the past hundred years.

A colourful display of instant baking products.

Shelves of salt containers and sauce and pickle bottles.

One section shows ten decades of shopping from the 1880s onwards. Another displays the rise and fall of the show-card, depicting evocative slogans such as 'Bovril prevents that sinking feeling'. The largest section of the museum covers the changes in packaging over the years.

Opie expands on the problems of selectivity and of where to draw the line. 'What I look for, for example, is the first milk bottle, and then for the first of a different type; for major changes in neck sizes and kinds of glass. I aim to encapsulate each commodity and to do it that way. Like that, you can cross-reference everything. For instance, if I'm doing the war period I've got the wartime bottle-tops that can be associated with salvage.'

The museum's war period is well represented by posters, pamphlets and all the paraphernalia that kept the family lively during dark war days.

One window is jammed with gas-masks, including an all-in-one baby-mask and a Mickey Mouse one with a red nose. These masks are backed up with instructions on how they should be fitted and have unnerving notices cautioning that 'Hitler won't send any warning'.

The tale is told of how wartime manufacturers adapted to produce emergency substitutes, gas-proof tea and liquid silk-stockings for ladies to paint on their legs. One enterprising firm even came up with 'Nasti toilet rolls' – 'Use Hess paper for mess paper' – and Izal issued rolls with ditties on each perforated sheet:

> Hitler now screams with impatience,
> Our good health is proving a strain.
> May he and his Axis relations
> Soon find themselves right down the drain.

Robert Opie believes that 'people who collect things often restrict themselves to date, size, or to a certain type of object, and so tend to pare themselves down. With stamps, the archetypal collection, collectors start off by searching for everything; then they can't cope and find themselves specializing. By the end of the day they're specializing in one sort of stamp which you look at through a magnifying glass and it's only of interest to about one other person. It becomes boring, and that's what I'm trying not to do. I'm trying to go outwards. What I'm studying is life and how humans live, so I'm always expanding.'

Tea packets from the 1930s and 1940s including some of the developing design of Typhoo Tea.

A bearded and bespectacled bachelor in his late thirties, Opie's white smile and energetic enthusiasm are as arresting as his achievements. He started to build his collection when he was sixteen. 'I was in Inverness,' he explains, 'unwrapping a packet of Munchies, when I suddenly had a blinding revelation. It struck me that if I threw the packet away I would never see it again and, if the manufacturers changed the packaging or went out of business, the 1960 Munchie packet would vanish for ever. From that instant I have saved everything.'

One of the things Opie is trying to do is to elevate industry to a place alongside the arts and sciences, so that when a child is at school he is directed towards all three. He wants to improve the standing of industry: 'After all, this country survives on it. We're no longer an agricultural society. There is nowhere in Britain where you can see how business has grown up over the past two hundred years or why it's important to make a profit, and so on and so on.'

Opie's is a collection of design relating to commerce, and he hopes that the interest, meaning and importance of it within his 'nucleus collection that is immediately understandable' will fill a gap in our museum world. Another of his aims is to make people appreciate how much more leisure-time we have nowadays and how much drudgery has disappeared from the life of the housewife.

For Opie the project is not just a hobby. It is a mission; a record of design, technology and social history. 'Museums don't really study this. If you go to the Victoria and Albert Museum you only see the most important things – the best productions rather than the everyday ones.'

Opie concedes that although he leads an interesting life his enterprise causes tremendous problems with logistics, finance and storage – and he is haunted by the knowledge that he must, continually, be missing something. 'I know that I'm not collecting *all* the contemporary things. I couldn't. Just England. I need some restrictions.' He smiles resignedly in among the Bisto, Oxo and Reckitts Blue. Endless people lend a hand, but it's difficult for him to go away for any length of time as he's building up so many little nucleus collections within the whole. He hasn't gone into machines yet, for want of space, although he has all the catalogues and hopes eventually to recreate entire shops.

Robert Opie's mother, once she had got over the shock of learning of her son's life quest, was anxious to help. In order to give himself more time for collecting he decided not to go to university, but he did take a job as a market researcher. Later he gave this up because he wanted to concentrate on setting up the museum. In 1978 a small part of his collection was exhibited at the Victoria and Albert Museum, but Opie realized that if the subject was ever going to be comprehensively treated he would have to do it himself. The Gloucester project is the first step along the way.

Besides packaging and advertising Opie is interested in magazines, 'because they deal with aspects of social history. Also greetings telegrams, newspapers and tickets. What I'm hoping to do is to create whole areas so that one can see the complete setting in which people used to live.'

When and where, in Opie's view, did packaging begin?

He sees it as having started when goods were issued with a brand name – 'particularly when they became colourful and were sold individually rather than being scooped out of some larger container into a paper bag'.

Robert Opie considers the supermarket to be the great unsung phenomenon of our time and one which has evolved very quietly. He goes round supermarkets most days of the week. He has little spare time. 'Most people who do this sort of thing have to be entirely dedicated. It's difficult for a "normal" person to understand the passion. Objects are a part of our lives. If you're a smoker and you happen to buy a packet of cigarettes you may have that particular packet on your person for several days; then the packet changes and it's gone. Something that has been part of you – a friend that has helped you through life – has disappeared. There is so much bias in records. Photographs, for example. Ninety-nine per cent of them are of weddings, parties and special moments. How many photographs are taken of people getting up, shaving, and so on? These moments go unrecorded.'

One vitrine is devoted to picture postcards. Opie outlines his views on this part of the collection. 'A lot of people just collect postcards. The way that I collected them, when I did, was to take a few main themes. I was interested in the history of the postcard, the earliest ones and then the later developments – something out of every category, so that you bring it right up to date and get the whole story of the postcard. A lot of people collect cards because they've got cathedrals, or animals, or birds on them. Well, I don't think that's collecting postcards. It's simple to do it that way because they're an easy shape to keep. I ask, "What has man made out of the postcard?" There have been ones with records on them, ones with feathers, jokes, and so on. I take a complete view of what the postcard has claimed in our social history. What has it meant in our lives? At one time, before the advent of the telephone, it was an actual way of communicating. You could write one in the morning and it would be delivered the same day. Tremendous history lies in that fact. The postcard part of my collection overlaps with the wartime part. I might have a hundred collections that all tie in with each other – as do the sections on games, jig-saws and music-covers, for instance.'

Opie earns his living by hiring objects out for films, TV and other purposes. He has no sponsorship whatsoever and thinks that proving himself will be a long process, maintaining that he's got to step up his collecting if he's going to reach his target by the age of ninety. And now he's only thirty-eight.

Snowshill Manor

—CHARLES PAGET WADE—

Charles Paget Wade, architect, artist-craftsman, collector and poet, died in 1956 and is buried in the churchyard in the village of Snowshill, Gloucestershire, within strolling distance of the Cotswold manor (now the property of the National Trust) where his personal collection is housed. This includes English, European and Oriental furniture, musical instruments, craftsmen's tools, toys, and a magnificent display of Japanese *samurai* armour arranged by Mr Wade to give the impression of a company of warriors meeting in the gloom with their weapons, banners and sacred objects.

J. B. Priestley describes a visit to Snowshill and its owner in the Jubilee edition of his memoirs, published in 1984:

The owner then, in the most charming fashion, conducted us over his house. He did not live there but in the outhouse. The manor itself he now used as a sort of museum. The inside was as crazy as the outside and as beautiful in its own way. We looked into ancient dim panelled rooms, in which were collections of spinning wheels, sedan chairs, model waggons, old musical instruments (you ought to have seen the wood serpents), and blazing lacquer from Peking. One room was filled with old costumes, cupboard after cupboard of gowns, crinolines, uniform coats, bonnets, beaver hats, cockades. You could have dressed whole opera companies out of that room. I have never seen such a collection outside a public museum. He then took us over the outhouse, where he had his bachelor living-room and workshop. They looked at first glance like the early illustrations to *The Old Curiosity Shop*. It is only those Dickens illustrations that can give you any idea of the amazing litter of things in these queer ramshackle rooms. There were tools and implements of every kind, coats-of-arms, skulls, black leather folios, painted saints, colossal tomes of plainsong, swords and daggers, wooden platters and I know not what else. Neither in one house nor the other did I catch the smallest glimpse of a modern book or newspaper or anything else

that belongs to our own age. The twentieth century was nowhere in evidence and the nineteenth had only just dawned there.

Charles Paget Wade's coat-of-arms bore the motto *Nequid pereat* ('Let nothing perish') and his passion for collecting began when, at the age of seven, he saved his pocket-money (a penny a week) and embarked on the buying of curios. This mania was triggered off by a Cantonese cabinet owned by his grandmother, who only allowed it to be opened and inspected on Sundays. The cabinet that intrigued him and led him to his overwhelming desire to possess examples of craftsmanship can be seen today among Yomud tent bags and rhinoceros-horn cups in a ground-floor room at Snowshill Manor.

The long-haired, sunken-cheeked eccentric in his wide-brimmed Tennysonian hat and black cloak, with his passion for practical jokes, must have cut a strange figure. Queen Mary, visiting Snowshill in 1937, commented that the most remarkable thing about the collection was Mr Wade himself.

In 1945 Wade wrote:

I have not bought these things because they were rare or valuable – there are many things of everyday use in the past of small value but of interest as records of various vanished handicrafts. What joy these old things are to live with, each piece made by the hand of a craftsman. Each has a feeling and individuality that no machine could ever attain . . . A room can be filled with innumerable things and yet have a perfect atmosphere of repose if they are chosen with thought and care to form a harmonious whole. The furniture should not stand out as a series of silhouettes but should merge into the background, the highlights being sufficient to show its form. This collection, not a museum, will be a valuable record in days to come.

This prophecy proved more than accurate. Today visitors pour through the crowded house. Each room

Opposite: An attic in the new south front houses the transport collection,
including boneshaker bicycles, baby carriages, model coaches and measuring wheels.

*A remarkable collection of suits of Japanese Samurai armour of the
seventeenth to nineteenth centuries, arranged by Mr Wade as a gathering of warriors
in the gloom, with their weapons, banners and sacred possessions.*

Opposite page:

*Above: A selection of musical instruments, strings grouped on the left, woodwind on the right.
In a small orchestra or band the brass and percussion would be to the right of the woodwind.*

*Below: The Seraphim Room. On the table are Persian lacquered boxes and pencil-cases.
The two cabinets, in the background, are from Spain.*

possesses a name chosen by Mr Wade and bearing some relation to its contents, decoration, or position in the house.

The contents of the manor were collected between the years 1900 and 1931 (at which point Wade handed them over to the National Trust). He was lucky to have inherited a fortune from his father which enabled him to amass his treasures.

While living in the old house in the courtyard, which stands today exactly as described by J. B. Priestley, Wade spent many of his working hours restoring and arranging the rooms in the manor. It amused him to think that he didn't have to pay rates on Snowshill as it was classified as unoccupied, although this did not prevent him from bedding hapless guests down among the eerie objects crammed into every corner of the manor house.

Besides writing volumes of verse and making comprehensive inventories of his collection, Wade wrote copious reminiscences of his life and work. He named these volumes *The Haphazard Notes*, and among them is a piece on the subject of collecting:

Great has been the delight of forming the collection at Snowshill Manor, an enjoyment of many years for I started at the age of seven. Collecting gives such a wonderful opportunity for a wider view of humanity, both the present and the past. How varied are the traits of those met with when searching for 'finds'; from most of them something is to be learned. How much to study, learn and discover of the years that have passed. How much of trades, crafts and materials, and of the works and traditions of many nations. How much more interesting any object becomes with sufficient knowledge to suggest how it was made . . . To how many interesting, strange, out-of-the-way places collecting has led. To old cities, markets, sleepy country towns, peaceful remote country villages at home and abroad. To all kinds of queer places, by narrow alleys, up obscure yards, to old inns, coach-houses, stables long disused, scrap-iron yards, ship's chandlers, sheds by watersides, old maltings, mills and barns. To old tumbledown sheds patched and propped with dim mysterious interiors heaped high with cobwebby accumulations of ages . . . To workshops of the saddler, wheelwright, blacksmith, baker, druggist, confectioner, carpenter, and to the watchsmith's little den behind his shop where many hoards of his father and grandfather still remained . . . To the cottage of an old weaver who made the finest silks and velvets for the Coronation robes of Edward VII – a craftsman of the highest skill . . .

Mr Wade's enthusiasm was boundless.

Charles Wade first saw an advertisement for Snowshill Manor in *Country Life* when he was serving as a sapper during the First World War in France. As soon as he was discharged he visited it and found that it had not been sold, spoilt or modernized. He bought, restored, filled and embellished it – laying out, with the help of M. H. Baillie Scott, the eclectic compartmentalized garden that, with its arts and crafts mannerisms, is faithfully tended today. Ponds, terraces, sundials and model cottages are laid out among thriving Irish yew walks. Wade, with his feeling for and love of colour, painted outside windows, downpipes and water-butts a smoky blue verging on turquoise.

Obsessed with theatrical effects, Wade liked to fill the great hall of the manor with smoke that belched out both from the massive fireplace and from his own cigarettes. The atmosphere had to be hazy and dramatic, and caused his friends to rub their smarting eyes.

It is not easy to describe in these pages the wonders of the harvest so lovingly gathered at Snowshill Manor. It is unique, and setting and contents perfectly complement one another.

Vintage Cameras
and Magic Lanterns
—CHRISTOPHER PETERSEN—

Christopher Petersen describes collecting as a disease that afflicts those in search of detailed information, and he should know as he has suffered from it on two separate occasions. As a boy he collected hundreds of vintage cameras, mostly from jumble-sales, dustbins and charity bazaars. Often they were being thrown away and Petersen felt compelled to 'save them from the grave'. Even his father, who for many years ran the Royce photographic business at Paignton, would laugh at him for hoarding junk. However, when the time came for Petersen to buy his first house these cameras came into their own as he had to sell his valuable collection in order to put down a deposit.

Above: Christopher Petersen holding a 1908 Sanderson half-inch plate field camera.

Examples of classic photographica, encompassing the period 1860 to 1960.

A few years later, when he was organized, he started again and now has over a thousand cameras, the earliest dating from 1860. These range from the earliest models to huge Victorian portrait cameras on mahogany tripods, early movie-making equipment and even a photographic 'gun' used to train First World War pilots.

Among many petrol-driven magic lanterns Petersen's favourite is a small metal box with a chimney on the top; the chimney allowed smoke to escape from the candle that provided the light for the show.

Petersen was fortunate that when Henry Wykes, a well-known Devon photographer and portrait painter, retired, he was able to acquire most of his photographic equipment, including a large wooden plate camera of the 1880s (which had been in daily use for ninety years), together with numerous plate backs, lenses and shutters, as well as a special soft-focus lens, for flattering portraits, together with its front-fixing, roller-blind shutter. As well as all this, Petersen bought Henry Wykes' darkroom equipment, his copying camera – a 10 by 8 inch Meagher for copying prints where no negatives exist – his walnut-stand half-inch plate camera by Perkin, Son and Rayment, together with its wooden tripod and three lenses, including telephonic and wide-angle, and a converted Bennethink camera used for press work.

Now Petersen 'just cannot stop collecting. Each stage leads to another. When I get a 1931 model, for example,' he explains, 'then I have to have the improved model of 1932; then 1933, and so on. There's no limit.'

Petersen has over 30,000 photographic objects, including a number of early flash-guns. One of these, *c*.1910, was wound up with a key and worked on similar lines to a cigarette lighter with flash powder.

Now Christopher Petersen hopes to open his own photographic museum at Bowden House, near Totnes. This eighteenth-century manor house was advertised in an estate agent's window ten years ago. Petersen, who was then working in his father's photographic business, spotted the sign and, together with other members of his family, bought it and saved it from dereliction.

In his proposed museum Petersen plans that members of the public will be able to dress in costumes of earlier times, provided by the management, and take photographs of each other that will later be printed in evocative sepia tones. Besides this engaging gimmick he hopes to reconstruct a full-sized Victorian darkroom and gas-powered cinema, for which he has, ready and waiting, twenty-eight 1910 cinema seats. One of his aims is to allow visitors to 'get away from the shelves and to touch and fiddle around with the cameras – at any rate the more robust models'.

Meanwhile solid teak cameras, early Brownies (in a variety of unexpectedly bright colours) and minute pocket cameras crowd cabinets and all other available space.

Outstanding amongst the exotic array is Arthur Newman's personal 'Nydia' camera. This carries a formidable description: 'A small bellows, collapsible, pocket-sized, twelve-shot, leather-bag, change-magazine, glass-plate camera of fine quality, fitted with a Ross lens'. This was Newman's favourite camera and it remains in good working order.

Another notable section shows Les Allan's original equipment, including his grandmother's chair – once used as a tripod. Les Allan, a movie pioneer, was not only the creator of Britain's first animated cartoon, but also invented the multiple camera. Many examples of his original artwork, showing how a cartoon is made up of individual pictures on cells, are on display at Bowden House.

Christopher Petersen acknowledges that the Royal Camera Collection in Bath is probably more extensive than his own, but points out that 'so few of the items are on show there at the same time that I think my own personal collection will easily rival it'.

Lawnmowers

—CHRISTOPHER PROUDFOOT—

Christopher Proudfoot's work at Christie's auction-rooms in South Kensington brings him into constant contact with objects related to many of his pet subjects: musical-boxes, gramophones and phonographs (about which he has written a book), carpenter's tools and early kitchen gadgets. Lawnmowers, on the other hand, are less likely to turn up in the saleroom. Proudfoot, who has been collecting these machines for about ten years, describes them as 'big, bulky and dirty; not the sort of thing antique dealers want the bother of handling'.

One very big shed in the Proudfoots' Kent garden shelters most of his fifty-odd lawnmowers; the others are dotted around in various out-houses, and the garage is 'full of a Daimler that hasn't been on the road for fifteen years. I go for anything that's old and useless.'

One of the things that appeals to Proudfoot in accumulating lawnmowers is that there are not many other collectors around: 'It is not yet a commercial field, which makes it more fun.' As a child he lived in the country and always liked lawnmowers, indeed

he took to everything old and mechanical, and so he had looked out for them for some time before spotting and buying his first one at a country-house sale near Tonbridge.

The very first lawnmower was invented in 1830 at Stroud in Gloucestershire by a man called Budding, who took the idea from a machine that cut the nap on cloth. The principle was a simple one – just a rotating cylinder of blades working against a fixed one – and the mower of today still works along the same lines. Up to 1830 lawns were cut by a line of men with scythes and only the rich could afford to maintain a well-kept stretch of grass. Such things didn't exist in cottage gardens. The largest of these new machines were drawn by horse, pony or donkey, depending on size, and this custom continued well into the present century.

Christopher Proudfoot puts many of his mowers to practical use. Most of them are in working order and he finds that various types of mower are suitable for the different kinds of task imposed by the state of a particular lawn, the length of the grass, and so on.

Opposite: Christopher Proudfoot at the 'helm' of a 1926 Atco, among mowers from the 1880s to the 1950s.

Above: Green's 'Supreme', a late 1920s, slightly updated version of a design going back to the 1860s.
(The grass-box is not original.)

Size, too, was a factor – 'one machine might be more appropriate for a main lawn, another for a little bit of side lawn'.

Although there are many toy lawnmowers on the market, Christopher Proudfoot's four-year-old son prefers the full-size models. Mrs Proudfoot isn't so fascinated by lawnmowers but she is extremely interested in gardening. Her husband considers that they are an ideally matched pair – he's not remotely keen on growing plants but likes to mow the lawn, while his wife looks after the flower-beds. They had to leave their first house when they ran out of space: he wanted to keep on enlarging the lawn and she wanted to increase the size of the beds.

Many of the mowers in the Proudfoot collection are surprisingly brightly coloured. Victorian ones were often painted a brilliant red or green with the lettering picked out in gold. Proudfoot says that fashion and individual taste came into it. 'Each make had its own livery which tended to change from time to time. Nowadays when one comes across them they have usually been repainted or have rusted, so that people assume they were always meant to be dark in colour. I've seen them finished in stove black. I've had all mine repainted in their original colours.'

In the matter of mowers, Christopher Proudfoot finds it difficult to know where to draw the line. He tends to be rather choosy about models made after 1950, but last year he bought a new nylon-line trimmer which will eventually become part of the collection. He is not, however, interested in remote control for mowers. 'I don't like electronics. I go for gear-wheels and so on – not for electric things. That's why I collect old gramophones. I don't have a hi-fi or even a video recorder. Ideally I try to make all my mowers work, but in practice I tend to acquire them rather faster than I can repair them. One of the reasons why I don't go for motor-mowers is that I don't have the time. They take an age to dismantle, whereas hand-mowers are much simpler – although even a very straightforward hand-mower in need of a repaint and overhaul can demand three days' work; nowadays I seldom have three days to spare.'

Proudfoot has an encyclopaedic knowledge of the lawnmower. He explains that 'the very first one was a two-man job. It was pushed from behind, and sometimes a helper had to pull from in front. Apart from their steel blades, all Victorian ones were made of cast iron and are very heavy as a result. The great change that has taken place in the twentieth century is that they have become very much lighter.'

Some of Proudfoot's early examples measure a mere six inches in width. 'No one wants a six-inch mower today when a twelve-inch one will do the same job far more quickly. They were once very useful for the narrow paths that used to run alongside borders.'

Among the owner's favourites are a pair of small border-mowers, both Victorian. One is English and, as well as being green in colour, was made by a firm called Green. It was their cheap model, made in cast iron and very heavy for its size. The other, also a six-incher and probably not much later in date, is American and is called a New Excelsior. It still boasts its original paint, which is unusual for a machine of that age. The Americans were the first to make their machines lighter and easier to use instead of concentrating only on durability.

Although lawnmowers very seldom appear in paintings, a picture of a man pushing a grass-cutting device (true to the eighteenth-century tradition of showing some action in foregrounds) did come up in a recent Christie's sale and Christopher Proudfoot was very tempted to buy it. He put in a bid but unfortunately missed it.

He does collect photographs of lawnmowers, advertisements from old magazines and original sales catalogues, and is building up a library of literature on the subject. He also occasionally comes across little cast-iron plaques that were once attached to the handles of some of the cheaper mowers. 'Unfortunately they didn't get going until the beginning of this century, but they're quite fun and I have several of them.'

Christopher Proudfoot is particularly fond of a machine engagingly named the Shanks of Ivanhoe. 'It was one of two that I bought in a country-house sale and that got the collection going. It is dated about 1930 and is fairly sophisticated. It's made largely of cast iron and has an ingenious machine gear-box. The eight blades in the cutting cylinder mean that it gives a pretty fine cut. It is useful for mowing tennis-courts, bowling-greens and things like that rather than for your average domestic lawn.' The Shanks of Ivanhoe is in working order and is in regular use on the Proudfoot lawns in Kent.

Curios

—JAMES REEVE—

James Reeve was born into a family of magpies. Parents, aunts and grandmothers were surrounded by paraphernalia.

As a child, Reeve set out to collect different types of fur. No visiting sable was safe. The hobby entailed snatching strands from the coats of his mother's friends. In order to secure his quarry he would have to creep down from the nursery, steal up to a furry pile in the hall and tweak out great tufts.

One of the objects which formed the nucleus of Reeve's collection is a strand of the rope with which Crippen was hanged. It hides in a tiny drawer below the miniature figure of a swinging man. James Reeve was given it at a children's party when he was seven.

A table had been laid out with presents from which the young guests were to make their choice. As soon as Reeve saw the sinister prize he coveted it and, a collector in embryo, procured it.

Wood Tenement, four ancient thatched cottages making up one long narrow house, nestles in a valley on the edge of Exmoor and is, according to its owner, 'horribly haunted'. With its low beams and bumpy walls, it is an appropriate repository for Reeve's collection which reflects his taste for the bizarre.

James Reeve maintains that one of his reasons for collecting is that friends are tempted to bring him presents – 'My collection of clockwork toys was partly contrived for the sake of my poorer friends.'

Above: James Reeve seated at his easel in the studio.

A collection of snakes with a snake-patterned stool, designed by James Reeve and embroidered by his aunt.

Shelves crawl with tin crocodiles, rabbits and mice. Reeve prefers the Japanese models: 'English and American ones tend to have eyelashes and whiskers that I have to paint out.'

Among the marvels in the kitchen–dining-room is a powder-horn from Rajasthan, a creature masquerading as an iguana (lurking under a table) and a quadruple mouse-trap from the Simpson Desert. Nearby is a tin of elephant's meat in gravy from South Africa. Reeve reads serving suggestions from the label: 'Vegetables and spices to your own taste please'. There is a tin of cobweb spray which he squirts into corners to keep his daily up to the mark.

On a desk in the blackberry-coloured library squats a hairless baby monkey. James Reeve looks at it closely. 'Something very peculiar has happened to its private parts. The cotton wool's coming out. It be-

longed to a great-aunt of mine. She must have been odd.' Beside the monkey stands a pickled hand in a glass dome, the subject of a strange episode in family history. Reeve's two sisters claimed to have explored further up the Amazon than anyone had ever done before. During an expedition, one sister foolishly drank some river water and, in a state of hallucination, alighted on a spit of sand and waved the boat away, whereupon a posse of Portuguese nuns emerged from the jungle. They had turned native after working for a mission that had been disbanded. Reeve's sister remembers the nuns as being bare-breasted, with wimples tied round their middles, and busily involved in cottage-industry: bottling hands to sell as souvenirs. It isn't clear whether these hands are those of monkeys or humans, but when Reeve was given his it was hairless

Shells and branches of coral in the bathroom.

and its nails were short. Now it is covered in hair and the nails are quite long. One day, Reeve fears, 'it will break its bonds and scrabble up the stairs behind me, like the story of the monkey's paw'.

Wood Tenement also houses a large collection of snakes, stuffed and otherwise. Lifelike china snakes from Botswana and a vast Portuguese python, made of porcelain and found by Reeve's aunt in the display-case of a jeweller in Old Lisbon, curl up with beaded adders worked by Turkish prisoners. A dried snake's skin (with which guests are expected to rub themselves down after bathing) hangs over a trellised screen in the bathroom. Tapestry stool-tops, embroidered by the aunt who brought the python back from Old Lisbon and designed by James Reeve himself, look particularly lethal: snakes emerge from the eye-sockets of ivory skulls to mingle with branches of coral, shells, pearls, dried flowers, and collages of butterflies and beetles.

On the dining-room table two negro heads with lolling tongues roll around in the company of a bosomy black china lady cradling a sailor on her lap. Among these stands a realistic toadstool of papier mâché, with roots and clinging tendrils; nearby is a half-eaten, soft-boiled, plastic egg. James Reeve takes this on his travels. In out-of-the-way places, such as the Arabian Desert, a joke can break the ice.

Among the silver lustre, Chinese supper service, witches' balls and glittering theatrical headdresses, it is not easy to decide where to rest the eye. In a spare bedroom a stuffed ferret, on the verge of swallowing a mouse, stands predatory upon a shelf, happy to share its home with weaver birds' nests plucked from bamboos, cases of stuffed wildfowl and a scrawny rubber chicken hanging from a hook.

James Reeve was once a monk. The Lord called him on the Madrid underground, where the stations are named after painters. Between Goya and Velasquez Reeve received his summons; he says that 'it must have been a crossed line'. He joined an order that ate little and spoke not at all. He found he had to go into the garden to feed himself with mulberry leaves. Before being driven out by hunger, Reeve lay in the monastery in a poor state, half-starved and 'dying of brucellosis'. He was given a pile of maga-zines to pass the time, one of which was an issue of *Country Life*. That issue contained a plea for someone to provide a home for an old staircase. In his delirium he wrote in, and later heard that a long-distance lorry filled with dismembered staircase had arrived at the home of his parents. He cleaned the staircase up and had it turned into furniture: book-cases with barley-sugar pillars, and decorative urns that were once newel-posts. The staircase had originally been carved by a pupil of Grinling Gibbons and articles have since appeared in *Country Life* demanding to know what has become of it.

Among the variety of ghosts said to haunt Wood Tenement is that of an Elizabethan woman who simply utters the Shakespearean equivalent of 'Have a good day'. Some occupants have heard a great cacophony of noise sounding like a celestial cocktail party. The still-room is particularly haunted and James Reeve doesn't linger in there. The boiler room, in which neighbour Auberon Waugh was circumcized, was once the surgery of the previous doctor owner.

From the house you step across a windy path between beds of herbs and wild strawberries to the studio where Reeve paints with hand-made sable brushes (reminding him, no doubt, of his childhood passion) beside a skull wearing a mortar-board. Near him stands another skull picking its teeth with a lobster claw. Propped on an easel stands a painting of a courtyard owned by a carpet dealer in Fez.

Besides painting, travelling and caring for his house, garden and many treasures, James Reeve is an incomparable cook. He owns a large variety of Victorian cooking utensils, including an ancient gadget for preparing Devonshire Potatoes. He has 'something verging on a fetish' for enamel cooking equipment and hangs his *batterie de cuisine* around a hexagonal waist-high pillar, its top used as a chopping-board, cribbed from one he saw in an old farm-house in Majorca. This he had made when he lived in London and was short of space. Above it, a Staffordshire font is nailed to the wall.

When making a bread-and-butter pudding Reeve insists that, as well as placing the dish in a bain-marie, it should also be wrapped in several sheets of newspaper. I can vouch for its perfection.

Opposite: An assortment of curios on the desk in the drawing room.

The Insolt Collection
—STANLEY SHOOP—

'Insolt' is an acronym from 'I've never seen one like that'. Any item it might describe is likely to be an unusual version of something that would otherwise be labelled as humdrum.

Suspended beside the door of Stanley Shoop's Elstree house is a nameplate that reads 'Sands'. This does not mean that the occupants are dreaming of a far-off beach. It should be read as 'S and S' – Stanley and Sandra, Sandra being Stanley's wife.

Once inside 'Sands' it is hard to believe that there is room either for them or for their three daughters, so defiantly do insolts jostle for space.

At first sight it is not easy to decide just what it is that one should be looking at, and this, according to Stanley Shoop, is the main point of his collection. Mr Shoop tracks down mysterious objects – the more mysterious the object the greater the pleasure he gleans from the detective work involved. The challenge is to discover intriguing stories behind the finds.

Normally one would not expect to be especially fascinated by a wages-book, but on inspecting one that is in the Shoop collection a visitor is likely to be surprisingly affected. Faded ink reveals that it was once the book of a British slaver plying between Liverpool, West Africa and Jamaica. Of the thirty-seven crew members, eleven died at sea, seven died in Africa and one in Kingston. Eight were press-ganged on to a ship that fought at Trafalgar, two deserted, six were discharged in Jamaica, and only the Captain and one crew member were left to tell the tale. Stanley Shoop also has the papers relating to the sale of possessions of the dead on behalf of the next-of-kin, and he considers it to be the most moving document in naval history.

Stanley Shoop with items from his collection. On the floor is a wooden-handled mould for making shortbread and on the table one of his favourite mystery objects: a cylindrical container – possibly an early nineteenth-century flame-testing apparatus.

A clapperless bell, a dog made up of Wills Woodbine packets, an unassembled telescopic scientific 'kettle',
Zulu snuff bottles, antique Chinese spectacles, a bull nose-leader, a clockwork watch demagnetizer and
an early exposure meter sitting on a copy of 'Expediency and Morality in Welsh Dress'.

Another of Mr Shoop's favourites is a book called *Expedience in the Morality of Welsh Dress*. 'Open it!' he instructs excitedly. 'If I'm correct, this is the book that was carried by Peter Sellers in the film *Only Two Can Play*. It was obviously made for a film as opposed to a play; only a film-maker would go to the expense of having dummy library labels printed for close-ups. It's simply a book that's been doctored. Look!'

The hallway at 'Sands' is hung about with insolts: mechanical pacing-sticks, a dog made entirely from strips cut from Woodbine packets, an object dubiously identified as a 1920s pogo-stick. Other oddities line the walls where visitors inch through to the sitting-room, which also has its share of mysteries.

Beside the model of a man, fashioned in nuts, bolts and springs and poised for a tooth extraction, hangs a poster of Queen Victoria printed for her Golden Jubilee. From a distance it looks much like any other poster, but on close inspection one can see that the outline is made up of words spelling out personalities and events important in her life and reign.

Largely on the floor, but also on every available surface, curious objects proliferate. Ancient Chinese spectacles, wooden scissors (identified as wasp-tongs), and a bell from the time of the great plague of London. In each case the example is an unusual version of its type. 'If I have a bell it's a different type of bell. If I have a laundry-marker then it's an unusual type of laundry-marker. Familiar things in unlikely versions. That's the common factor. If it's a book then it's an unusual book or it has an unusual title.' Here he pulled out a copy of a book with the title *Rules to which an Assistant Executioner is required to Conform*, and another called *Extraordinary Popular Delusions in the Madness of Crowds*.

Stanley Shoop admits that his collection is highly subjective and accepts that it might not be of interest to anyone else. For him, the pleasure of his style of collecting lies in what he's going to get out of it afterwards. He bases the cost of a purchase on its subsequent entertainment value, paying for ingenuity and design rather than for precious materials. His eyes are always open, although he has to consider space and fears that the time has come for him to face up to weeding out a little and improving the quality of his collection. It would be very hard to make a decision on the dispensability of a Japanese fly-trap, a Victorian hanging gold-fish bowl, a 1930s sun-ray lamp or a minuscule safety-razor.

The Shoop collection started with books about forty years ago, although stamps were his first love. His wife Sandra joins in only to a minor degree but now manages to tolerate the confusion in the house. At one time it did drive her crazy but, although she sometimes makes a face about it, she now stomachs it and cooperates. Certain aspects of the Shoop family's life-style are necessarily dictated by the insolt passion. Two telephones from a diesel train are installed, one at each end of the hall, so that the children can communicate. Invalid bells have been fitted and reversed to summon the girls from their bedroom when they're playing records upstairs.

About once a year *Country Life* publishes a photograph of a mystery item from the collection in the hope that one of their readers can identify it. Stanley Shoop is always keen for help in matters of identification and is overjoyed when people come up with helpful suggestions. The mysteries that are bugging him in particular at the moment have defeated a great many enthusiasts. Top of his list is a cylindrical container, once nickel- or chrome-plated. This has baffled everyone at the Science Museum. Fixed to the bottom of a snug-fitting stopper is a stiff wire ending in a small loop. What is it for, and how old is it?

Another teaser is a brass and bakelite object with a base and two discs which are capable of rotating through 360°. Could the use have anything to do with electricity? Is there any significance in the fact that while one side of the discs is plain the other has a brass bar across it? Perhaps the bar is there to support the discs?

He held up a brick-sized object, also made of brass and with two sets of taps on either side of a knob in the middle which gives access to a central compartment; the back is marked 'Generator only'. It could possibly be something to do with a very early motor-car, but Mr Shoop just doesn't know.

One of the joys of insolting, Stanley Shoop explains, and one of its chief attractions, is that it is left entirely to the collector to decide where to draw the line, so that each insolt collection is different and can truly reflect the interests of its compiler.

Advertising Fans

—*JANET STREET-PORTER*—

The writer and broadcaster Janet Street-Porter lives at Limehouse with her third husband, film director Frank Cvitanovitch, in an early Georgian sea-captain's house which commands a spectacular view over the river to the Surrey and West India Docks. The only disadvantage to this otherwise unrivalled position is lack of privacy on the river side. Tour leaders, guiding visitors through London's waters, can be heard announcing, 'That is where Janet Street-Porter lives', as they point in the direction of her balcony.

Janet Street-Porter already had twenty years of collecting behind her when she bought the house, which is dominated by her interest in art deco, the fashionable style of the inter-war period. Her husband, at the time of their marriage, had thirty years of collecting blue-and-white china, Napoleonic swords and military watercolours behind him. They got rid of the swords and found that the blue-and-white didn't go with art deco, so that stays in their country house. Their next joint collecting venture is to be built round Victorian Gothic.

As an offshoot of art deco, Janet Street-Porter has collected advertising fans since 1966 when she went to an auction at Christie's and coveted a shoe-box filled with them. Bevis Hillier (whose book on art

Opposite: Janet Street-Porter with her collection of fans spread over a 1927 walnut veneer table at Limehouse.

Above: Detail of an art deco advertising fan.

· 119 ·

deco she had given 'a really bum review') topped her bid and she was very cross. Later, to her astonishment, he went round to her Chelsea flat and presented them to her. 'He's that sort of person. Very spontaneous. He said that I should have them. That was how it all started. There were about five fans in the shoe-box and since then they've been exhibited in Minneapolis in the first really big exhibition of art deco in America.'

Janet Street-Porter joined the Fan Circle for a bit. It is a group of rather up-market ladies who collect fans, but only about half-a-dozen members collect advertising fans. These are absolutely the only fans that interest her. One of the reasons why she left the Fan Circle was because it was too closely connected with major auction houses, so that 'what started as a nice little thing got a bit ominous, and fans began to go for way over what they were worth'. It's difficult to find bargains in England now, but oddly enough she has bought several in America and Australia.

The fans constitute a collection within a collection and, as in the décor of her house, she doesn't restrict herself strictly to date but goes for what she calls a 'certain look'. All the fans have been made for specific events. Stores such as Galeries Lafayette would have, for instance, a 'Fur Week' and fans would be printed as give-aways. Others have come from Paris hotels, Frascati's, Zandra Rhodes and Royal College fashion shows.

Janet Street-Porter spread her fans out on a 1927 walnut veneer table (part of a suite made for Jack Cohen, Tesco's owner). The fans are not normally on show but live behind glass. They are extremely fragile and people are tempted to handle them. The idea is to have, one day, a black lacquered room where they can be more easily seen.

She only bothers to sleuth the earlier fans. New ones 'just come along' – sometimes as hand-outs on aeroplanes. She will only buy a fan if it is in excellent condition. The same rule applies to everything in the house. She cannot bear anything to be out of place and hates smokers (although she does love ash-trays).

Among art deco lamps, screens from Derry and Toms and cushions covered by herself in Zandra Rhodes off-cuts, friends can walk warily over a brightly coloured carpet designed by Patrick Caulfield to look like a swimming-pool. Pictures on the wall are modern and painted almost exclusively by artists she knows: Jim Dine, Alan Jones, Caulfield and Hutto.

She fiddled with Susie Cooper pottery pieces on a table behind the Eileen Gray sofa (colour faded by the sunlight that battles through double-glazing). One or two objects were out of place. Everything has to line up. 'It's a bit worrying to be like that, I know,' she confessed, flashing a toothy smile. Were it not that words flowed from her lips in such an uncontrived and friendly fashion, it might have been tempting to wonder whether her inimitable cockney accent is assumed.

As in the case of many collectors, space is a problem. Besides being immaculately tidy, Janet Street-Porter is a terrible hoarder. The kitchen, leading from the sitting-room but entirely disguised by splattered cream and orange paint which looks like the shell of a tortoise or the coat of a leopard, absorbs a mass of art deco teapots which mostly came her way as presents from friends after her book on British teapots was published. Other objects are kept in the cellar: 'It's like an old people's home down there . . . lots of things just resting.'

Miniature Models of People

—HUGO VICKERS—

Unlike many collectors, Hugo Vickers has no cause to sigh after treasures that have given him the slip. He has complete control over his collection because he created it himself. In his London flat he has at least five hundred intricate models of famous people who were alive at the time their replica was made.

The hobby started when, as an Eton schoolboy, Vickers made a model of St George's Chapel, Windsor, which he loved and knew well. He commandeered a large attic room at his home in Hampshire and spent nearly every waking hour in it during the school holidays. After the chapel came the occupants. He started by making deans, canons, members of the choir and military knights, and then added Knights of the Garter and members of the Royal Family. From there he went on to fashion a variety of other figures, his choice partly dictated by whether he thought they would be fun to make. 'It was very enjoyable doing a Field Marshal, for instance,' he said, picking up a small frowning figure. 'I like him.' Another favourite is the Emperor Haile Selassie, with his scarlet uniform and Garter ribbon.

Side by side on a table, in great numbers, stood Admirals of the Fleet, Generals, Marshals of the Royal Air Force and others, all accurately attired in appropriate uniforms. 'Particularly inspiring,' Vickers remembers, 'at a big service at St George's were the amazing Greek Orthodox priests – archimandrites. They wore marvellous robes and they had big black beards. Anything like that I'd enjoy doing.'

In the school holidays Vickers would often work hard to depict two or three particular events in the chapel's year. The Garter service took a whole summer (that of 1968) to assemble – stitching at robes for the twenty-four Knights and others, working from photographs or from memory. On one occasion he devoted twenty-four hours to the Yeomen of the Guard and, although it was wonderful to have them afterwards, he says he has never been so bored in his life as he was in the making of eight identical bodies and thirty-two arms and legs. They were complicated to construct because of their intricate uniforms, but the only real fun involved was in adding the odd moustache or pair of spectacles.

The models, which stand between four and five inches high, are made out of cardboard, crêpe paper, pins (an astounding number of these), scraps of material, cotton-wool and other oddments. Hugo

*Above: Emperor Haile Selassie of Ethiopia in the uniform of a British Field Marshal
with the Emperor Hirohito of Japan and his wife the Empress.*

Vickers must have presented an unlikely figure as a schoolboy scouring the remnant counter of John Lewis. 'I used to annoy assistants by asking for half a yard of this or that, but my friends were very kind and presented me with items from their boxes.'

Hugo Vickers drew attention to a figure slightly larger than the rest. 'Here's the Archbishop of Canterbury. Now he's probably the most intricate and one of the last I ever made. He was sewn by hand – sequins all over him. Material for the faces was either white or pink according to the effect I wanted to produce. When I made Harold Wilson I wanted him to look a little bit soft and pink. If I made an older person – like him' (here he pointed to the uniformed effigy of Lord Mountbatten), 'I made the face white. It was easier to draw on. I drew in the faces with a ballpoint pen and then put on cotton-wool hair. Sometimes I used fake hair from a switch I found in Woolworth's. You could get them in different colours.'

Lord Mountbatten was made, as were most of them, between the years 1965 and 1969. He was revised on 11 September 1970. All such details are meticulously chronicled below each figure.

Speaking with the passion of commitment, Vickers says that as the collection expanded he made lists of the figures he still had to construct. 'Having done the Knights of the Garter and their wives, I thought that I'd put in all the widows as well. I discovered an extraordinarily obscure widow of a Knight, so I made her.'

This 'extraordinarily obscure' widow was Gladys, Duchess of Marlborough. Some years later Vickers wrote a successful biography of the forgotten lady which came about as a direct result of having made her likeness. There were always a number of people on Vickers's conscience: people who needed to be 'done'. He would feel guilty if he discovered that he had misrepresented somebody: 'If I saw somebody in real life and found that my model wasn't a good likeness, then I would feel in duty bound to remedy it; I would be inspired to do better.'

Vickers has recently written a biography of Cecil Beaton. 'Unfortunately I never made one of him. I ought to do one just for fun. It would mean breaking the rule that I must stick to living people. I was thinking the other day that it would be amusing to do. I'd probably be rather dramatic and put him in a white suit. He would have his CBE round his neck – even if he does wear a scarf. He would wear his clothes, as he always used to do, slightly too tight.'

On the table stood a veiled figure dressed in black. 'That's the Queen of Denmark, Queen Ingrid. She's another of the last ones I made. When King Frederik died there were pictures of Queen Margrethe, Prince Henrik and Queen Ingrid at the funeral. I love mourning. It's so dramatic. I used to line them up and form processions. It was great fun. I would whip up a lot of people quickly for a funeral and then play around with them later.'

Behind Vickers and above the sofa where he was sitting hung a framed heraldic document. It had taken him three weeks to make. First he settled down and made all the coats-of-arms of the Knights of the Garter to go round the outside and then he forged all the signatures in the centre. I asked him how he had found the real signatures in order to copy them. 'Well, I also collect autographs. I wrote for them all . . . Some of them were a bit surprised. I copied them out – a warning to anyone, I suppose.'

Hugo Vickers, with every justification, claims to have invented the style of his models, but admits he was influenced by a visit to Madame Tussaud's as a child. 'Mine are caricatures in a way. They are meant to be funny as well as lifelike. I learnt a great deal from it – about ceremonial and so on. I gave up making them because it was important for me to go out into the real world. It was an enjoyable teenage hobby; obsession, perhaps. Better, I thought, than hanging around discos, smoking pot or whatever.'

I asked Hugo Vickers if his peers had ever found it bizarre that he should have been occupied in this way. Displaying disarming trust in human nature, he replied: 'Well, if they did they were very nice. You know how people are. I don't think that I was ever teased about it. There were some rather unsympathetic neighbours who said things that annoyed my parents, but after all I was living in a world of fantasy. Absolutely. I think that it was a creative fantasy, but, well, it's hard to explain . . .'

Opposite: Hugo Vickers with his models.

Model Ships and Aircraft

—SIR PATRICK WALL, MP—

Sir Patrick Wall shows enthusiasts round his collection of model ships and aircraft with the gusto of a schoolboy but with the knowledge of an experienced historian. Three rooms, the great staircase and a hallway of his house in the north of England are given over to his collection, which spans the whole spectrum of ships from Alfred's long-boat to the Polaris submarine. Not only do they cover all eye-level surfaces, but they also occupy the space overhead. Aircraft models are suspended from old clothes-drying pulleys to which they are attached by barely visible strands of dental floss. Sir Patrick explains that if he had put the aeroplanes on shelves, those shelves 'would have to be a mile long. This method is pretty effective and, although they do get dusty, you can't see it. I think it gives a good idea of the various aircraft and how they developed.'

He started to collect model ships at the age of eight. In those days a firm in Wales made metal models. They were rather like Dinky toys, and he remembers purchasing them as a child. When the war came, he already owned a model of practically every type of warship from the major navies of the world. 'These models,' he says, 'were not too bad, but nothing in comparison with those of the present day.'

By the time Patrick Wall went away to school he was making his own wooden ships (a hundred feet to the inch) and the collection includes the first, now somewhat battered, example of his early work. At Downside he and a friend were given a spare dormitory by the headmaster of the time in which they could play various kinds of war-games.

In 1935 Patrick Wall left school and went into the Royal Marines, in which he was to serve for sixteen years. He took with him, even during the war, his collection of ships. By this time he had also started collecting merchant ships. There used to be a shop in High Holborn that sold magnificent models of liners for about £5 each. These can still, from time to time, be bought at auction, but for very different sums from those of pre-war days.

After the war Sir Patrick Wall began to go beyond the hundred-feet-to-one-inch scale and embarked on collecting bigger models. The largest now in his possession, the passenger ship *Southern Prince*, was presented to him by the Sea-Scouts. It had been kept at their headquarters, but these were broken into so frequently and the model, glass case and all, had been so badly damaged that the Scouts asked Sir Patrick (who had been President of the London Sea-Scouts for many years) to take it away for its own safety. It is about twelve feet long, its winches exquisitely turned by apprentices, and is a beautifully made maker's model. It takes its place in this representation of the entire history of world shipping – the first Nile papyrus boat; the first sailing boat; on through the ships of the Phoenicians, Greeks and Romans, to the castle ships and beyond.

Sir Patrick's collection is a part of his own absorption in naval history and it is hard to believe that anything can be lacking; but gaps can always be filled by the commissioning of a model. He now has one example of every class of ship in the Soviet navy. He also has a unique collection of landing-craft made for him by 'a chap called Glossop. He later became a model-maker for the Admiralty. He's dead now, but his son has taken over and most of my recent models are made by him.' He doesn't know how many ships his collection comprises but he thinks it must be well over 6,000.

Over the years he has acquired a great many plastic models. Whenever he goes abroad he will hunt for these, admitting that 'many people disdain plastic but, well made and well painted, I think that with some of my better examples you can barely tell the difference between plastic and wood.'

The three gems of the ship collection are to be found under glass on the upstairs landing. All three

Opposite: Sir Patrick Wall with military aircraft models.

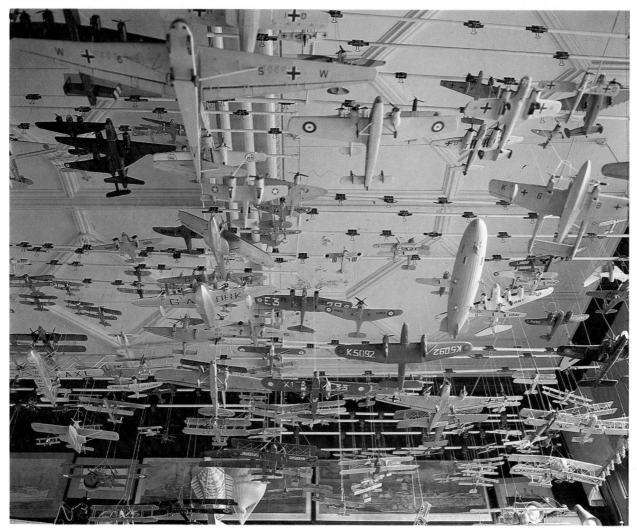

Above: Part of Sir Patrick's fly-past, which ranges from balloons to spaceships.

Opposite: Model ships with aircraft of the Fleet Air Arm overhead.
The large liner is a model of the 'Southern Prince'.

were made by a Yorkshireman. The first is of the *Dreadnought*, the very first British battleship of the First World War. Sir Patrick describes it as 'a beautiful model. Look. It has oars and everything. Those black marks on the deck represent the scuttles where they used to push in the coal.'

Having acquired the *Dreadnought* he commissioned a model of the *Vanguard*, the last battleship to be built. This ship, on which Sir Patrick served as Second Gunnery Officer, is constructed to the same scale as that of the *Dreadnought* and the pair show very clearly the difference in size between the first and the last battleships of the First World War. The

Vanguard, too, he considers to be perfect. 'It's even complete with seagulls' – these gulls fly in the air above the deck, supported by near-invisible wire. He regrets that the *Vanguard* has had to be scrapped: 'I wish we'd kept her, as the Americans did with theirs.'

The third of these particular gems is a model of HMS *Valiant*, on which Sir Patrick served for the greater part of the Second World War. He spent eighteen months on her in the Mediterranean and in the Indian Ocean; he was also with her at Salerno and during the invasion of Sicily, as Captain of Marines and Second Gunnery Officer in charge of four or five

guns. On this model puffs of smoke, made from blackened cotton-wool, belch from barrels; this was done as an experiment as Sir Patrick wanted to see the guns firing. He remembers sitting on the main turret as the Italian fleet, on its surrender, came into Malta. He can even pinpoint his own cabin on the bridge.

On shelves lining the stairway visitors pass more model ships: that of Christopher Columbus; the vessels of the Armada; the *Victory*; the *Clairmont*; the *Great Eastern* and the *Great Western*; the *Titanic*; even the *QE2*.

At the bottom of the stairs Sir Patrick points out a 'sea-effect ship'. This is the American development of the Hovercraft. It is an experimental model and is now in the process of being built. Sir Patrick explains that while our Hovercraft has a flexible skirt, the American version has a solid one. 'It can't go up on the beach but comes alongside, and it goes anything up to about seventy knots. The trouble is that with the first experimental one so much fuel was needed that it wasn't feasible to run it. Now they're finding a way round that problem.'

Ships were his first love; aeroplanes came later. The entire Fleet Air Arm flies above the heads of visitors. These planes are mostly made of plastic, but some are of balsa wood. This section starts with balloons and ends with spaceships, taking in along the way the very first monoplane, flying-boats and Sea-Harriers. He doesn't go in for commercial aircraft, but to date he has about six hundred military models.

These jam-packed rooms, with all their contents chronicled, dated and described, are as neat and cared for as those in any small museum. The walls are backed with trophies from their owner's travels – wooden masks from Africa, coolie hats, carved animals and ancient weapons.

When you ask Sir Patrick Wall if he considers himself to be an expert in his field, he replies, 'I've always been interested, and I have a large library for reference. It embraces everything about warships and merchant ships, and has some rare books. I should think that there must be about 8,000 in all. They are being catalogued just now.'

Sir Patrick Wall imagines that the aim of every collector is to make sure his own collection is complete, although he ruminates a little gloomily on the future: 'What happens when I finally depart this life I don't know. The Maritime Museum won't be terribly interested since they haven't any more space than I have. Heaven knows if my grandchildren will want them; it's certainly not very likely that they will have room for them either . . .'

Brass Musical Instruments

—JOHN WEBB—

John Webb's collection of over two hundred and fifty brass instruments, the earliest dating from the eighteenth century, is kept in glistening condition at his secluded Wiltshire house. He describes his passion for them as 'a case of Trombomania, an acute form of Trombophilia, which has, in its chronic state, a

deleterious effect on normal human relationships – particularly those with bank managers'.

Webb considers the disease to be particularly Anglo-Saxon in origin. He knows of one other case in the British Isles, a few in Germany and Switzerland, several in North America, and none in France or

Above: A selection of hunting and orchestral horns.

Italy. He says that 'in its incubation period the patient is merely aware of an obsessive interest in the sound and look of trumpets. As it develops, this infatuation tends to embrace all brass instruments. The pathology of the disease is uncharted. Most Freudians would agree, however, that the trumpet is a symbol of masculinity and therefore of virility. It is an appendage to the extrovert. It denotes amplification of the voice, domination of one's fellows and a childish gratification of aggressive instincts. It is flashy and somehow more glamorous than the violin or flute.'

In Webb's case, symptoms began when he was three. He was absolutely fascinated by trumpets. By the age of ten the condition was fully developed and he was driven to join the Boys Brigade in order to get his hands on one.

At that time most Boys Brigade companies had bugle bands. During his recruitment interview Webb couldn't take his eyes off a row of battered trumpets hanging on a rod in the Captain's office. He remembers the interview well: 'The Captain, a sensitive man, stuck a mouthpiece in one so that I could blow it. The lovely shiny tubing was heavier and colder than I'd imagined, and sounding it was not the simple skill of my fantasies. Nevertheless, within a few weeks I was playing in parades, swaggering about in a web of tassels and dress cords and telling others how they should be blowing.' The prognosis was hopeless.

Not one of Webb's friends shared his interest and he looks back upon it as a lonely business. 'For a long time I was alone with my affliction, self-conscious and furtive, haunting instrument shops, boring people, reading about trumpets, thinking about them, blowing and buying them. Many of the trumpeters I met seemed to be trumpeters by accident. I couldn't understand why they weren't also automatically interested in keyed bugles and early valve systems.'

It is surprising that a man as quiet and gentle in manner as John Webb should have developed a

John Webb holding the silver slide-trumpet that belonged to Thomas Harper Sr, Sergeant Trumpeter to Queen Victoria. On the floor, surrounding him, are ophicleides, and on the wall are, from the left, trombones, keyed bugles, flugel horns and trumpets.

mania for so much noise. For a few years he was able to contain his condition sufficiently to earn a living in another sphere of activity, but during this period collecting old instruments became addictive: cornets, saxhorns, ophicleides – anything and everything – had to be possessed. He thinks back to the time when 'a blackened, dented bugle in a sale-room was enough to cause a quickened pulse-rate and shallow breathing; then euphoria or delirium. Metal tubing glimpsed in a junk-shop window would have me hurrying across a street to be confronted by a bundle of curtain rods. Travelling round Europe for my "fixes", the narcosis could only be assuaged by playing, this time the trombone – bigger, grander, louder than a trumpet. I settled on the biggest, grandest and loudest of them all – the bass trombone.'

Webb has many theories about the musicians who play the instruments that affect him so profoundly and believes that brass-players are a particular type. 'They conform. They cling together and have little to do with other players in the orchestra. They used to be regarded as rough, as having beery breath and overt heterosexual proclivities. Violas viewed them with distrust bordering on fear. Brass-players did not have the sequestered sensibilities of flautists and oboists. They were loud and cynical, slightly unstable and potentially dangerous. Trumpet-players were regarded as neurotic (although opinions differed on whether they were neurotic to start with or whether the trumpet made them so). No other musician had to play a case of instruments which were constantly exposed, constantly transposing, subject to all the vicissitudes of lip, spit and nerves, even temperature. Trombonists, on the other hand, were more solid. They sat around, legs apart, placidly counting bars, sniggering occasionally at private asides, watching their fellows with a touch of mockery. Conductors and all other musicians have constantly complained that the brass play too loudly.

The truth is, of course, that they are the voice of denouements, crises and climaxes. This has never gone down too well with wind- and string-players responsible for hours of frustrating foreplay. They're jealous, that's all.'

Meanwhile, John Webb's collection is, he says, far from complete. He still doesn't have a keyed trumpet (a circumstance he continually bemoans). He has eight ophicleides but no bass horn. He allowed a German ophicleide to go to someone else at auction not long ago and 'hasn't had a wink of sleep since'. He has three serpents but no continental one; he did, however, get a curious French cornet with revolving pistons last Christmas. He doesn't have a Sampson valve instrument, or a Nuremberg trumpet. A curator known to John Webb recently acquired a sonorophone, and Webb 'hates him with a vehemence that I didn't know I was capable of'.

There was a time when he used to find one or two instruments a week, but now they are very scarce and he's lucky if he gets one or two a year. One of his favourite possessions is an ophicleide that was found in the loft of what had once been a music-shop. Although completely black and with moth-eaten key-pads, it had never been sold and was essentially in mint condition.

Webb's interest, although passionate, is not restricted to the instruments themselves. Recently, with four other brass-players, he started the London Ophicleide Ensemble in which he plays a bass ophicleide. These instruments, Webb's favourites, were originally important components of the early brass band and were scored for by symphonic and operatic composers. They lingered on in decreasing numbers until the end of the last century.

Although John Webb restricts his collection to old instruments he has the greatest possible respect for many of the modern ones, finding them 'absolutely marvellous'.

Dulwich Wireless Museum

—GERALD WELLS—

Gerald Wells describes the vintage wireless museum at his home in Dulwich as 'not so much a museum as the manifestation of a psychiatric condition'.

He believes that a shock from a nursery wall-socket may have infected him with 'wirelessitis', for it seems that his mania began as soon as he was born. One of the most exciting periods of his mother's life was in 1929, when, within a few weeks of his birth, electricity was being installed in the house where Wells still lives. She followed the electricians around the house as they worked, and was fascinated by the whole process. Wells believes that that might have had something to do with it. Another possible explanation is that the house was previously owned by

Alfred Rickard-Taylor, one of the first radio 'hams', and that he may have left some electric vibrations behind him.

By the time that Gerald could walk he was tinkering with electrical things. 'In fact,' he says, 'I was a great problem to my parents. They thought that there was definitely something very, very wrong. I had a one-track mind. They were longing for me to go out and do all the normal things. My passion got me expelled from two quite good schools. I would do anything to get hold of electrical stuff. It led me into endless trouble.'

When he was two-and-a-half his parents took him to Margate for the summer holidays, but nothing

Mr Wells in the Daventry Room, named after the first Long Wave station,
surrounded by GEC, Bush, Murphy and Alba radios.

*Wireless sets from 1917 to 1930 in the Paul Getty Room, so-named because
John Paul Getty Jnr is a great supporter of the vintage wireless museum.*

held his attention until he reached the boarding-house where they were to stay. There he fell in love with a red light-fitting in the hall; he wasn't interested in the sea, the sand or anything else, and it drove his parents nearly mad.

He now realizes that it was 'definitely a mania; a fanatical craving for radio and electricity. Nothing electrical in the neighbourhood was safe, at school, at home – anywhere. In the end my parents allowed me to use a space at the end of the garden where bonfires were made. It was a good place to hide away from my sisters, who were older than I was.'

At nearby St Joseph's College Gerald Wells was not a success. It was a purely academic school, without so much as a science lab. 'Nobody had any sympathy with me and by the age of twelve I was expelled. I was completely isolated. Other kids were bored with me; adults too. Everybody found me a pain in the neck. I started removing radios from

bombed houses, even pinching things from shops and air-raid shelters. It was an overriding passion. After being slung out of St Joseph's I went before a juvenile court and was whisked off to Stanford House Remand Home. I stayed there for a fortnight, after which I was taken to a well-known psychiatrist. He was worse than useless and advised that the mania should be stamped out by sending me to a good boarding-school. With my reputation not one of them would touch me and I ended up at a council school in Brixton. That was all right, but there was no one there for me to discuss wireless with. I couldn't hold a conversation with the other kids because I spoke a different language. My head was full of radio. I've worked it out of my system now, but in those days I could think and dream of nothing else.'

Wells attended the Brixton School for long enough to earn himself a good character report and went on to the Brixton School of Building, where he remained

In a corner of the Droitwich Room (named after the Droitwich transmitter) is the Ekco section, with radios from the 1930s made by the company famous for working in moulded bakelite.

for seven months before trouble started again. This time, at the age of thirteen, he took a fancy to a radio in Archie Roots' shop in Norwood High Street. 'I did a little blag on that one Saturday afternoon. I rushed in and nicked it off the shop counter then pedalled away on my bike. I was caught by Archie Roots himself in his Austin Seven van. That, of course, meant severe treatment and I was sent to Stanford House again. During a fortnight's bail I was caught removing all the electrical fittings from an empty rectory, whereupon the juvenile court in their wisdom decided that I must be removed from everything electrical and I was sent to a farm school in order to lead an open-air life. On the 1st of January 1944 I arrived at the Red Bank School near Liverpool. On my third day John Varley, the headmaster, came up to me. He was a marvellous man. I told him that I had a craving for radio and he said "Have you now? Funny. I've got a member of staff with the same

trouble." I thought: Here we go. I'm going to have the mickey taken out of me again. So I took no notice. A few days later, after they'd found out whether I could read or write and what diseases I'd brought up from London, he introduced me to Reggie Yates. He was a Lancashire man and ran both the local and the school cinema. Together we set up a business. I was given a bike and access to local radio shops. I had the run of the place and I was into radio at last. It was my first break – marvellous.'

Later that year Gerald Wells was let out on licence. In the headmaster's words, 'There's nothing wrong with this lad. He just wants radio.'

Wells came south and was placed as an apprentice in a building firm. For three years he was allowed to tinker with radios to his heart's content; he made cabinets and undertook repairs for the staff. He passed his driving test and in 1951 he started doing trade work for Archie Roots – he even bought the van that had led to his arrest. He thought: Well, this car got me to Red Bank before so maybe it'll get me there again. 'This time I went as a visitor. Yates was still there and so was John Varley. We all set up in business together and from then on I did regular trips up and down to the school, helping on the staff – right up to the time when Reg Yates electrocuted himself on one of the television sets that I'd taken up there. He was killed outright. It was terrible. He'd been a good friend and mentor.'

The school asked Wells to take over Yates's job for a while, so for a few months he actually worked at the remand home where once he'd been an inmate. On the fortieth anniversary of his release he wrote to the school to say how much he owed them.

In 1957 Wells set up his own repair service, and it grew and grew. Now, in his late fifties, he owns over a thousand vintage wireless sets (all in working order) and works fourteen hours a day, seven days a week. Having left school at the age of twelve, he finds it an effort even to write the simplest letter. 'Academically I'm a disaster – but I owe everything to the Red Bank School. It was marvellous.'

Wells hopes that he is no longer looked upon as a crank; more as an authority. He takes tours round his museum and gives lectures, maintaining that he is as nervous as a kitten but 'I manage it somehow'.

The Dulwich house, heavily belled and wired, is a place of pilgrimage for enthusiasts. Today the bedroom of Wells's late parents is jammed with vintage radios, many of which were rescued from rubbish-dumps and dustbins. He thinks his mother and father would be pleased to know that 'everything has worked out all right in the end' – that after a long fight he has gained full support from friends, relations and the public at large.

The dining-room is full of pre-war television sets and Wells's own bedroom houses a radio transmitter that puts him in touch with 'the whole complex'. This consists of sheds at the bottom of his own garden and those adjoining it. Neighbours take part in any shows he puts on, remove sections of their fencing on open days so that festivities can run into three gardens, and provide him with space for sheds. In exchange he will build conservatories for them, convert lofts and tend their radio and television sets.

Radio is Wells's hobby, his job and his way of life. He owns a large library of manuals and books and by next year he will be the only person in the country manufacturing valves.

The most prized object in his vast collection is the tally number – 118 – from the Red Bank School. He retrieved it when he returned there as a teacher. It lies in a glass cabinet with a hand-written inscription. 'This single item,' he says, 'has more to do with radio than anyone could possibly imagine. When I write my autobiography I will devote a chapter to it.'

There can't be many gaps at the Dulwich Wireless Museum but Wells would dearly like to get hold of a Latimer radiogram as sold in 1934 by Whiteley's of Bayswater. He remembers being terribly excited at the age of four when his parents bought one. In the mid forties it was rebuilt and modernized, in the process losing its appeal. He could, of course, make a reproduction of it from memory, but it wouldn't be quite the same.

Most members of Gerald Wells's family worked in insurance and his eccentricity came as a great surprise to them. Although, he muses, 'there was Great-Uncle Alfred who sold toilet seats off the back of a horse; and then one of the great-aunts was Arnold Bennett's mistress . . .'